Live Butterfly
Activity Book

Activities, Suggestions, and Resources
For Teachers, Parents, and Kids
Using *Live* Painted Lady Butterflies from Insect Lore

Text by Robert Drake

Illustrated by Garth Bruner

Technical review by Carlos White, MS

Content and activities are based on the frameworks of the
National Science Education Standards and the
Head Start Program Performance Standards.

INSECT LORE

PO Box 1535 • Shafter, CA, 93263

www.insectlore.com

© 2002 Insect Lore • Printed in the USA

CONTENTS

Here's how to set up your 1-oz homes.

The kids see what makes a caterpillar a caterpillar.

A caterpillar has a good life inside a 1-oz cup.

In a few days, the caterpillars set growth records.

There are good reasons to be cold-blooded.

Instinct can save an interrupted meal.

A caterpillar's life isn't as easy as it seems.

Live Butterfly Activity Book © 2002 Insect Lore

CONTENTS

1 tsp sugar / ½ cup water

LAB FACTS

LAB SAFETY   Where lab safety is concerned, good lab behavior is a process or a series of related actions. Here are some lab safety suggestions that you might want to consider sharing with your students for *any* science activity. They're written with both a positive spin and simple ideas that most junior scientists can grasp, but feel free to translate them as necessary for your class.

- What Question
- What Tools
- Keep Track
- Keep clean
- Room to work

- Lab safety begins with knowing what question you're trying to answer by doing a particular activity.

- You know what tools you'll be needing for the activity and how to use them correctly.

- You keep track of all the little pieces and parts in your materials so you don't lose them and also to keep them away from younger children and pets who might try to chew on them or even try to swallow them and then choke.

- Next comes knowing that your lab area and tools should be kept clean before, during, and after the activity.

- You also know that running, playing, eating, and drinking are things you do elsewhere. You've given yourself plenty of room to work in so you won't be bumping into other people or equipment, too.

- Sometimes a scientist has to use fire in a lab. (NOTE: <u>None</u> is needed for any of the activities in this book, however.) Always have an adult present when fire is used in a lab and if clothes catch fire: **STOP! DROP! and ROLL!**

Your emphasis on lab safety is very important and the kids will catch on fast if they see you following the rules, too.

When you're nose-to-nose with the kids day in and day out, "administrative help" might seem like an oxymoron. In this case, however, you really *do* have help. Published in 1996, the NSES give teachers common goals as well as ideas to help get the kids there. The activities in this book have been organized to make it easy for you to find the science concepts and skills you want to teach and to include the content standards found in the NSES. You can read the full text of the Standards by going to *books.nap.edu/catalog/4962.html* which is the web site for National Academy Press. The National Science Teachers Association (NSTA) will also welcome you at *nsta.org* where you can buy your own copy of the standards plus lots more.

THE NATIONAL SCIENCE EDUCATION STANDARDS

In 1998, a legislative mandate provided Head Start with an important tool for teachers. The resulting effort became known as the Child Outcomes Framework which describes eight general Domains, over two dozen Elements, and a variety of specific Indicators of skills and behaviors for children ages 3-5. The Framework is intended to be used as a guide to help Head Start teachers to identify key building blocks that are important for pre-K children to have for school success and to suggest ways to include those building blocks in their lessons. The goal is to strengthen the quality, consistency, credibility, and assessment capabilities of local programs. With that in mind, Insect Lore drew from Head Start information to identify and include with the activities in this book the Elements and Indicators from the Literacy, Language Development, Math, Science and Approaches to Learning Domains found in the Framework.

HEAD START: CHILD OUTCOMES FRAMEWORK

Lab Facts

HMMM . . . Some teachers express concern (even fear) about presenting any type or aspect of science. The consensus seems to be that science is too difficult or technical, requires a huge amount of preparation time, and the outcome has to "work" just as the book describes. The biggest teacher issue might actually be the blank looks that sometimes follow what was thought to be a "great" lesson. So, what to do? The simple ideas that follow are suggestions to help teachers cope with these conditions.

COUNT
COMPARE
CLASSIFY
OBSERVE
MEASURE

Experts in such things have suggested that the basic skills to emphasize in pre-K scientists should be: count, compare, classify, observe, and measure. These skills seem to provide the best foundation so kids can move easily into more science areas and experiences as they grow. At early ages, the fact that a gas called carbon dioxide is released when you mix solid sodium bicarbonate and liquid acetic acid is less important than the fact that it just happens and that you can create the foamy, stinky mess anytime you want. Of course, the level of understanding you expect from your students should increase as they gain experience with variables, data collection, cause and effect, prediction, terms, and equipment. The pre-K focus, however, should be on the basic tools the kids have between their ears.

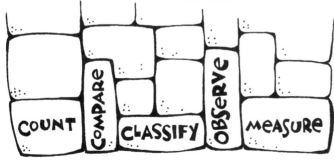

An easy acronym to keep in mind is <u>KISMIF</u>. It stands for: Keep It Simple, Make It Fun. The amount of learning that comes from a lesson is not necessarily linked to the complexity of the presentation. In other words, simple is often better. It's also a safe bet that if you're tired of or bored with a presentation, then the kids will be, too. Usually, it's easier to have a better teaching opportunity if the learning experience is simple and fun for everyone. It does need to be well-directed, however, and there's a simple learning model that can help you do just that, too.

KEEP IT SIMPLE, MAKE IT FUN!

Educators generally agree that "constructivism" is one idea that identifies ways to help achieve learning objectives for a lesson. In a nutshell, the idea is that people construct (or learn or "hook") new information on top of what's already known and/or familiar to them. New information is analyzed and compared to what's already in place. Then it's added as is, modified, or discarded because it doesn't make sense, i.e. there are no existing hooks for it. A lesson's goal should be to have everyone start at the same place, build the new information on top of what they already know, and to use pretty much the same hooks as everyone else. An easy way to help get the kids started at the same place is to give them some real experiences (or hooks) with what you're teaching *before* you actually try to teach it.

WHAT HOOKS?

LAB FACTS

A LEARNING MODEL

Reality Check: This is the ideal, of course. Usually, the demands of your schedule will limit just how much exploring and applying you can allow. However, it's very possible that these could occur after the kids have left your classroom. You're planting seeds.

A simple learning model to consider is: Explore—Explain—Apply. Traditionally, teachers present the vocabulary pages, work sheets, and reading ahead of an activity. Some experts suggest, however, to have the kids get into an activity and explore it <u>before</u> any reading or writing occurs. After the initial exploration, have them talk about what they saw and did. That gives them the hooks they need for the explanations you provide and those they discover for themselves. Then have them apply what they discovered by testing variables and new ideas. In other words, kids just want to <u>do</u> it, so have them Explore first. Let them see what happens and what changes. This accounts for the "Oh yeah! I saw that!" when you Explain what took place. Student pages, work sheets, vocabulary lists, etc. usually come with this discussion. Talk about "what if" and suggest things to do when they revisit an activity to Apply new ideas and test more variables. This approach can be used with each activity in this book and it fits with *all* of your teaching, too. Science is way cool and it should be a great experience for everyone!

LAB ANIMALS

Like lab safety, the humane treatment of animals in your classroom should be a no-brainer. Anytime you have animals in your lab (or class), they must be well cared for and treated kindly. Butterflies are ideally suited to classroom science for junior scientists. They're clean, safe, easy to care for, and very quiet (uh, the butterflies, that is). They are living creatures, however, and need some special consideration in a lab setting. <u>None</u> of the activities in this book (or the ones you and the kids dream up) should involve deprivation, extremes, or pointless destruction. The best example of treating lab animals with respect will come from you and, like the lab safety behaviors you demonstrate, your class will connect with what they see you do.

INSECT LORE

Insect Lore has been providing live Painted Lady butterflies to homes and classrooms for over 30 years. In that time, 3 versions of butterfly kits have emerged as the favorites. Each is available either with live caterpillars for immediate use or with a certificate to order caterpillars for a later time (kits purchased in stores have only a certificate, of course). The available kits are:

- Item #101, the Butterfly Garden, with 5 caterpillars
- Item #311, the Butterfly Pavilion, with 10 caterpillars
- Item #133, the Pavilion School Kit, with over 33 caterpillars

Everything you need is included in each kit so your experience with live butterflies will be totally successful. Insect Lore guarantees that you'll have at least 60% emergence of the adults but it's more likely to be 100%. The experience is truly amazing!

Each Insect Lore butterfly kit is a stand-alone experience and this book is not needed with any of them. However, all the activities in this book can be used with any of the three kits. You should know that the activities suggested here are based on the Pavilion School Kit and its 33+ caterpillars. Where necessary, the instructions for an activity have included any changes you might make if you're using one of the other kits. Regardless of which kit you use, the outcome will be memorable and exciting!

LAB FACTS

METAMORPHOSIS The experiences in this book use Painted Lady butterflies (*Vanessa cardui L.*, see page 83) and, unless the text says otherwise, the procedures, facts, and interesting details are specific to the Painted Lady. Working with live butterflies is truly a wonderful experience. In fact, after you witness your first emergence, you'll wonder why you didn't do it sooner. What was for you at first a tentative plan becomes an event the kids talk about all year. You'll also become more confident of your abilities and emerge from your own chrysalis of skepticism and self-doubt. You'll have undergone your own metamorphosis to greater confidence. Good for you!

KEY INFORMATION When an especially important piece of information is in the text, look for the butterflies in the margin next to it. This will help you quickly locate that fact you needed or remind you to stress an important point to the kids.

 This butterfly is in the left side margin.

 This one is in the right side margin.

RESOURCES In addition to over 30-years' experience, Insect Lore drew from the following resources to provide the latest facts, information, and ideas. Grateful acknowledgement is given to each author.

- Borror, Donald and Dwight DeLong (1976), *An Introduction to the Study of Insects, 4th Edition*, Holt, Rinehart, and Winston, New York, NY
- Flanagan, Tom and Carlos White (1971), *The Butterfly Curriculum, Activities for K-2*, [self-published] Insect Lore, Shafter, CA
- Kaae, Dr. Richard and Patricia Kaae (2000), *Travels With My Ant Lion* [a CD], Cal Poly Pomona, Pomona, CA (See page 62.)
- Mikula, Rick (2000), *The Family Butterfly Book*, Storey Books, Pownal, VT
- Schaffer, Donna (1999), *Painted Lady Butterflies*, Bridgestone Books, Mankato, MN

> *Kids probably know that having a pet means lots of responsibilities for someone (usually they think it's you at school or a parent at home, too). Living things have basic needs that must be met and butterflies are a great way to teach that fact as you and the kids create places for them to thrive.*

Content, Skills and Indicators—

1. environments, needs of living things, simple tools

2. measuring, following directions, observing

3. sees relationships, describes living/non-living things

Pavilion School Kit Materials—

- 33+ Painted Lady caterpillars (larvae)
- Specially formulated, ready-to-use caterpillar nutrient
- 33 1-oz portion cups with lids
- Plastic teaspoon
- Small brush

You provide:

- Student Journal page from this book (see pages 4 and 86)
- Tray or flat box to hold the cups
- Warm, dark, and undisturbed location

Other Insect Lore Butterfly Kits—

Butterfly Garden

There's no set up required for the caterpillars if you're using the Garden. One 8-oz cup has the food already in place for its 5 occupants. You do need a warm, dark, quiet location.

Butterfly Pavilion

There's no set up required for the caterpillars if you're using the Pavilion. Two 8-oz cups have the food already in place for the 10 larvae. You do need a warm, dark, quiet location.

TIMELINE:
Give yourself 20 to 30 minutes for the set up and about the same time for a simple lesson.

PREP NOTES:

1. Make sure hands and tools are clean and dry during the set up. Caterpillars can be sensitive to bacteria and excess moisture.

2. If your scientists are less than seven years old, plan on doing the entire set up. You may be doing it even if they're eight. It's your call—it's your class.

3. Your caterpillars will do better in a location that's warm (72°-78°F), reasonably dark, and not too disturbed.

4. Depending on temperature, the metamorphosis can take up to 3 weeks and the butterflies may live an additional 2-4 weeks. Plan your lessons so you're around for the emergence. Missing it is no fun!

HOMES IN A CLASSROOM

THE IDEA

A <u>Reminder:</u> These directions are written for the materials found in the Butterfly Pavilion School Kit and its 35+ larvae.

The kids will be very excited to care for their "own" butterfly so you won't have to hype this activity much at all. However, try to avoid getting your class too wound up before you receive (or even order) the larvae.

How you handle this set up is a function of several factors: the age of your kids, your teaching style, the time-line you face, and how much help you may have available. The caterpillars are reasonably hardy but you do need to transfer them to their individual cups as soon as possible after their arrival. Your choices to accomplish this include: (1) you do it all, (2) the kids do it all, (3) a third party does it all, or (4) a combination. The end result is that there will be 33 1-oz cups, each containing one caterpillar with some food on the bottom and a lid on the top. The two 8-oz cups (one had all food in it, the other had the caterpillars with food) can support up to 5 caterpillars each if there's about a half-inch of food remaining inside each cup and the paper liner under the lid is intact.

THE METHOD

Cleanliness means that you've washed and dried your hands, the tools you're using, and the surface on which you're working. But no, you don't have to wash each of the 1-ounce cups.

1. Keeping cleanliness and dryness in mind, find a work space where you have some comfortable elbow room and then separate the 1-oz cups from one another. Set them aside.

2. Open the large cup of food and, with the spoon, scoop a generous half-spoonful of it into a 1-oz cup.

3. Using the bottom of an empty 1-oz cup as a press, force the nutrient (food) firmly and evenly into the bottom of the loaded cup. Some water may be forced out but try not to squish out too much.

4. Each 1-oz cup needs a generous quarter-inch of nutrient in it, so adjust the amount you spoon into it accordingly. It's very important that the food be firmly wedged into the bottom of the cup so that it can't be dislodged as the larva moves over it to feed or if the cup is dropped. Do this to all of the 1-oz cups. You'll have plenty of food.

5. Open the cup of larvae and avoid tearing the paper liner as you remove the lid. Keep the small brush dry and use it to gently pick up <u>one</u> larva and transfer it to a 1-oz cup. See the margin notes on using the paint brush transport system. Set the lid back on the larger cup to keep the other larvae inside as you work. Hold the brush inside the 1-oz cup but don't touch the nutrient with the bristles. As you hold the brush with your thumb and index finger, flick it with your ring finger. The larva will drop safely into the cup. After you've placed a larva inside, snap a small lid in place. Repeat this until you've placed <u>one</u> larva in each of the small cups with nutrient and capped it with a lid.

It may be easier to move the larvae if you trim the tip of the brush slightly. A safe and effective way to move a caterpillar is to hold the brush nearly perpendicular to the body with the bristles under the head. Then, gently roll the brush so the top side of the bristles rotates away from the front of the caterpillar. The caterpillar's front legs will grab the rotating bristles and it will be safely drawn onto the brush.

The caterpillars (larvae) are small but they can move faster than you might expect! Placing them in a refrigerator for about 10 minutes slows them considerably.

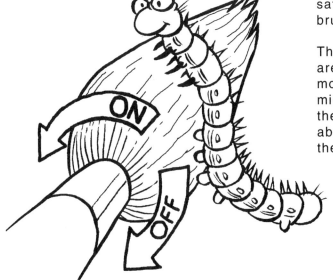

HOMES IN A CLASSROOM

THE METHOD

Each 1-oz cup has plenty of air for the larva so you <u>don't</u> need to punch holes in it.

The cups should remain warm, undisturbed, but <u>out</u> of <u>direct sunlight</u> as the caterpillars grow and molt. You can keep them covered on a tray or inside a box so the larvae are reasonably safe. It *is* important that the kids be able to regularly see inside and watch what's happening but jostling the cup (like taking it home) isn't a great idea. The larva should be as undisturbed as possible, so playing with it and touching it are on the "Uh-uh" list as well. Picking up the cup to get a better look inside is fine so long as it's not dropped or shaken (*or* stirred, for that matter).

A JOURNAL

Whether your kids are skilled readers or use books only as booster seats, you can help them get the most out of their experience with butterflies by having them build a journal or scrap book. This idea supports literacy, language development, observation and data collection, creative skills, organization, and (for you) assessment. To these ends, the student pages found starting on page 86 offer a great deal of flexibility for you and your junior researchers. If your kids can read and write, use the pages as you wish. If reading and writing are yet unacquired skills, get the sense of what the pages present, translate it for your little ones, and help them glean the key ideas. The whole point is to make the experience easier and more fun all around.

LESSON HINTS

• You'll want to resist the temptation to give names to the caterpillars or to identify a student as the "owner" of one of them. While the chances of survival are high, there is the possibility that "Wiggly" or "Tony's caterpillar" will die (see page 12) and then it can become a very personal issue for some kids.

• Show/find/discuss local animals and critters of all sizes and shapes that are available and in season. Remind the kids that it's safer to just look at insects. Use a hand lens or observation jar to see them up close. If you look at living locals, be sure to release them where you found them.

• Observe small animals that crawl and/or fly; compare/contrast the size, shape, color, number of body segments and covering, eyes (location and number), habitat (see page 17), number and type of legs, wings, etc. of insects (like butterflies, ants, flies, grasshoppers, praying mantis, ladybugs, etc.) with other arthropods (like spiders, millipedes, ticks, pill bugs, centipedes, lobsters, etc.—see page 83). See THE ARTISTS' MODEL on page 53 for more help with this comparison.

• See page 22 for suggestions about marking the cups to track increases in caterpillar length and size while watching the level of the food supply drop.

LESSON HINTS

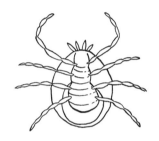

• There are many excellent connections in literature. Here are only a few:

The Butterfly Hunt, Yoshi, Picture Book Studio, 1990

The Girl Who Loved Caterpillars, Jean Merrill, Putnam, 1992

The Very Hungry Caterpillar, Eric Carle, Philomel Books, 1969 ⬅

Where Butterflies Grow, Joanne Ryder, EP Dutton 1989

Use the common misunderstanding found in Eric Carle's story to teach the kids that a moth makes a <u>cocoon</u> and a butterfly makes a <u>chrysalis</u>. Mr. Carle has graciously acknowledged falling into the trap.

• Consider the kinds of food animals actually eat ("Do caterpillars *really* eat holes in things like lollipops, sausages, ice cream, cupcakes, and Swiss cheese like the very hungry caterpillar?" Frankly, no, they don't but then, what *do* they eat? Most are very picky and will eat only one or two kinds of leaves.).

• Talk about the many responsibilities of caring for animals (providing the needs of living things: shelter, food, water, etc.).

HOMES IN A CLASSROOM

LESSON HINTS
• Lead the kids into what it might be like to watch "your very own caterpillar change into a butterfly." Help them see that real scientists also watch and take care of animals to learn new and wonderful things about living creatures. With very young children, you may need to help them understand that this natural process can take a long time (2-3 weeks) to complete.

• No matter which Insect Lore butterfly kit you're using (see page ix), make sure you and the kids will be around the whole time. A break in the school calendar longer than a weekend makes it tough to track all the changes. And you don't want to miss an emergence!

• You'll have more larvae than 1-oz cups. Not to worry! If there's about a half-inch of food on the bottom and the paper liner under the lid is intact, as many as 5 caterpillars can be in each 8-oz container.

WORD POWER
These are a few of the words and topics (hooks) you might want to have handy and use during this activity. Doing this could help keep everyone using the same hooks as the discoveries unfold.

butterfly

caterpillar

change

chrysalis [*krís-ah-liss*]

environment

growing / growth

habitat / home

insect

larva / larvae [*lár-vee*]

life / living

life cycle

living / non-living

Nature / natural

needs of living things

nutrient

observe / observations

Even though they're tiny at first, the caterpillars may elicit some big questions from the class. This activity should make your life easier (and the kids', too) by helping them identify what they see inside the 1-oz cup without having to check with you all the time. Well, that's the plan, anyway.

Content, Skills and Indicators—

1. characteristics, form and function, inquiry

2. observing, communicating, inferring

3. using senses and simple lab tools

Pavilion School Kit Materials—

- Individual caterpillar in a cup for each student

You provide:

- Opportunities to observe
- Student Journal page from this book (see page 88)
- Hand-held magnifiers (optional)
- Drawing/writing materials (optional)

Other Insect Lore Butterfly Kits—

Butterfly Garden

You have 5 caterpillars to observe in a single, 8-oz cup with the Garden. The kids can have a successful experience with this kit but you'll have to coordinate their viewing opportunities. A great deal can be learned especially if you're in on the observation. The cup can be closely watched but shouldn't be handled to avoid dropping it or warming it.

Butterfly Pavilion

There are 10 caterpillars in two 8-oz cups with the Pavilion. The suggestions made for the Garden apply here, too, but having 2 cups should make things like coordinating observation times a little easier.

TIMELINE:
You can have caterpillars to watch for as long as 10 days (depending on the temperature). Allow several minutes each for observation time and for the kids to make notes and pictures or to talk with you.

PREP NOTES:
1. You're not trying to make your kids into entomologists. You just want them to be comfortable using the correct terminology to describe what they see in the cup.

2. "Nothing is constant but change" and that's certainly true of a fast growing caterpillar. It gets easier for the kids to see and identify the parts of the caterpillar as it grows.

3. See LESSON HINTS on page 12 for ideas on handling the death of a caterpillar.

CATERPILLAR ID

THE IDEA
Depending on the age of your students and where you live, there may be some of them who have no idea what a caterpillar is and what it becomes. You may need to give them an overview of what lies ahead for the tiny wiggler in the cup so the kids know it's destined to be more than bird bait. This may also be the first time they've had animals in a lab setting so you'll need to make sure everyone is on the same page with respect to the treatment you expect for the caterpillars (see page viii). The focus of this activity is to put names to the various parts of the caterpillar so the kids can better describe what they see in the cup.

THE METHOD

1. You want good lighting into the cup but not so much that the contents get warm and cause moisture to condense on the inside wall of the cup (Remember: no direct sunlight on the cups!). If enough moisture forms to make a drop that dribbles downward into the droppings, you risk the growth of bacteria that can be deadly to the caterpillar.

2. For better viewing, elevate the cup to the kids' eye-level when they're seated at their lab station. Use a narrow but stable pedestal under the cup so the kids can easily see upward as well as downward into the cup. An inverted plastic tumbler, small mixing bowl, or coffee mug will work nicely. Something with some sturdiness to it is less likely to tip if it gets bumped by a stray elbow or a distracted hand.

3. Be sure to leave the lid on the cup and look closely at the caterpillar. If it crawls out of view, rotate the <u>pedestal</u> slowly to move the cup so the caterpillar can be seen more easily. The less anyone actually handles the cup the better, since that reduces the risk of dislodging the food, heating the inside of the cup, or disturbing the caterpillar.

4. The first few times they look at it, the kids may only see a blob of fuzz with few distinguishing features. Of course the size of the caterpillar will make a difference in what's visible but there's much to see even on the tiny versions. This is a great opportunity to use a hand lens for close up viewing. Ideally, each student will have a lens, but since this is real-world teaching, you'll probably have to review your most recent lesson on sharing. You can check out the LESSON HINTS on page 11 if you need to review the preferred way to use a hand lens.

THE METHOD

5. While you may not expect anatomical and/or verbal perfection from your class, it's certainly OK to expect them to be able to describe a caterpillar using accurate terms. These illustrations of 2-week old caterpillars can guide you as you help the kids connect names to the parts they see on their growing caterpillars. You'll notice that most of the protective bristles (setae) have been left off so the details are more easily seen.

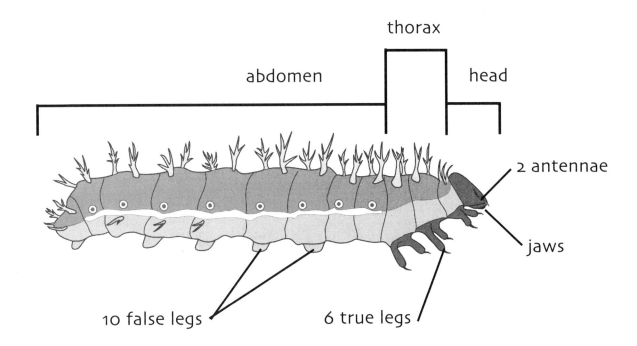

thorax

abdomen

head

2 antennae

jaws

10 false legs

6 true legs

CATERPILLAR ID

THE METHOD

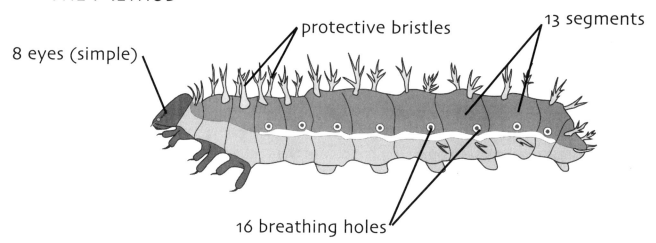

8 eyes (simple)

protective bristles

13 segments

16 breathing holes

LESSON HINTS

• While the focus of this activity is on the caterpillar and labeling its parts, there are some questions that inevitably arise about life inside the cup. Other activities will answer them in more detail but this may help for now.

"What's the green stuff on the bottom of the cup?"

Caterpillars are very finicky about what they eat; some more than others. Painted Lady caterpillars are not as fussy as most, however. This nutrient has been carefully developed over the years and is a combination of a plant called hollyhock, supplements, water, and other essentials.

"How does a caterpillar get air and water?"

They need very little oxygen and there's plenty even in the closed cup. Like some other insects they breathe through holes in their abdomen. Water is very important and it comes from the food they eat. Of course, too much water can be as bad as not enough.

"What are the green balls on the bottom of the cup?"

Like all living things, caterpillars poop and it's called "frass." At first it's tiny, light green, and scarce but gets to be huge, dark green, and abundant as the caterpillar grows.

"What are the fuzzy black lumps on the bottom?"

To grow, a caterpillar sheds its old, small skin and grows into a new, larger size. This is called molting and the black, fuzzy balls are the cast-off old skin (see page 35).

• For older kids, there are more technical terms you could use to identify the parts on the caterpillars, e.g. the eight bead-like eyes are ocelli [*oh-sél-eye*], the protective bristles are called setae [*sée-tee*], and breathing holes are spiracles [*spéar-uh-kuls*]. Adjust the vocabulary to fit the level of your expectations.

• An important point you could teach with this kit is how to use a hand lens correctly. This may be the first simple lab tool some of your kids have used. If they're just looking at and not writing about or drawing what they see, then have them hold the lens in a writing hand about 8 inches from their eyes.

To enlarge and focus the image, tell them to either (1) lean slightly toward or away from the subject moving the lens and their body together keeping them about 8 inches apart; or (2) move the lens slowly in and out until the largest, in-focus image is achieved with the lens about 8 inches from the face.

Some kids try to plant the lens on an eyeball and then expect to actually see something. This option doesn't usually work as well. Sometimes closing the weaker eye (the non-writing hand eye) may help them concentrate better on what they're seeing.

CATERPILLAR ID

LESSON HINTS

• At Insect Lore, over thirty years of effort has gone into making sure all of the caterpillars become butterflies and 60% are guaranteed to do so. Sometimes, however, Nature pulls a fast one and a caterpillar dies. Where there's birth and life, there's also death, a natural part of the process. You may want to discuss this possibility in advance with the kids and have some lessons ready that deal with life cycles, living vs. non-living, habitat changes, or environmental influences on life. In most cases, the School Pavilion Kit provides more than enough caterpillars to fill in for any premature departures. Most students are OK with this possibility, too, especially if they've been made aware of it. If a caterpillar dies, it's best to toss the entire <u>unopened</u> cup into the garbage. If there's a bacterial infection involved, you don't want to risk passing it on to the other caterpillars.

WORD POWER

These are a few of the words and topics (hooks) you might want to have handy and use during this activity. Doing this could help keep everyone using the same hooks as the discoveries unfold.

abdomen
breathing holes
false legs
focus
jaws
ocelli [*oh-sél-eye*]
protective bristles
segments
setae [*sée-tee*]
spiracles [*spéar-uh-kuls*]
thorax

> *The kids will be drawn to the small cup to watch the caterpillar living inside. You can enhance this natural curiosity with careful observations to make the most of the opportunity, too. The best part is that you can do this no matter how old the kids are or which Insect Lore kit you're using.*

Content, Skills and Indicators—

1. organisms and environments

2. observing, collecting data, investigating

3. awareness of living things and the natural world

4. compare, measure

Pavilion School Kit Materials—

- Individual caterpillar in a cup for each student

You provide:

- Opportunities to observe
- Hand-held magnifiers (optional)
- Drawing/writing materials (optional)

Other Insect Lore Butterfly Kits—

Butterfly Garden

You have 5 caterpillars to observe in a single, 8-oz cup with the Garden. The kids can have a successful experience with this kit but you'll have to coordinate their viewing opportunities. A great deal can be learned especially if you're in on the observation. The cup can be closely watched but shouldn't be handled to avoid dropping it or warming it.

Butterfly Pavilion

There are 10 caterpillars in two 8-oz cups with the Pavilion. The suggestions made for the Garden apply here, too, but having 2 cups should make things like coordinating observation times a little easier.

TIMELINE:
You can have caterpillars to watch for as long as 10 days (depending on the temperature). Allow several minutes for observation time and for the kids to make notes and pictures or to talk with you.

PREP NOTES:

1. It's obviously more difficult to observe tiny caterpillars but it's important to start as soon as possible so the kids can see the huge growth that takes place inside the cup in a very short time.

2. As the kids become more skilled, they'll find more and more details in less and less time.

3. If you have the kids make drawings, it's OK for them to be generally accurate and not necessarily precisely correct.

Micro-"Habitats"

The Idea

If you wish to, and your kids have the capability, this activity can become a very real lab experience. Even if they're non-readers, very young, or don't have much lab savvy, you can help them start to build valuable habits for future lab work. The goal here is to see more than just the caterpillar and to notice how it impacts the environment in the cup. Help the kids understand that following a definite plan or procedure each time they work in a lab is a good idea (especially in your crowded classroom). For example, having them use the same spot in the lab each time they make an observation, using the same lighting for each observation, storing their materials in a certain location, or talking with you about the new things they saw are ways to build good lab skills.

Keep in mind that disturbing (shaking, dropping, touching, etc.) the caterpillars isn't a good idea at all. Of course observing them (looking closely) is fine.

The Method

A hand lens (magnifying glass) is an optional but valuable tool. See page 11 if you're not sure about the way the kids should use one.

1. You want good lighting into the cup but not so much that you warm the contents. Above all, keep the cup out of direct sunlight so it doesn't warm up and cause moisture to condense on the inside wall of the cup.

2. If possible, elevate the cup to the kids' eye-level when they're seated at their lab station. Use a narrow but stable pedestal so they can easily see upward as well as downward into the cup. An inverted plastic tumbler, mixing bowl, or coffee mug will work nicely.

3. Leave the lid on the cup and look closely at the caterpillar. If it crawls out of view, rotate the <u>pedestal</u> slowly to move the cup so the caterpillar can be seen more easily. The less anyone actually handles the cup, the better.

4. The first few times they look at it, the kids may only see a blob of fuzz with few distinguishing features. Of course the size of the caterpillar will make a difference in what's visible but there's much to see even on the tiny versions.

5. Building on what they did in CATERPILLAR ID on page 7, have the kids note the changes in the caterpillar's general physical size, colors, appearance, appendages, etc. Then have them get close enough to watch how the caterpillar eats or moves. Some may even see a molt in progress (see page 35) in a resting caterpillar. While younger researchers will have a harder time with such details, even they can be guided to discover much of what's happening in the cup.

6. An important part of this activity is to note the other changes that are occurring inside the cup. Things like the amount and location of silk (see page 38), quantity of food remaining, patterns of eating, size and color of the frass, discarded molts, etc are major influences in this micro-"habitat."

7. Have the kids develop patterns of observation, e.g., check their latest drawing or digital photo first for a reminder of what the caterpillar used to look like; start looking at the same end of the caterpillar each time they observe it; draw a new picture and compare it with the old ones; talk with you about what they saw, etc.

Micro-"Habitats"

Be flexible in what you expect from both your kids and yourself in terms of observed and recorded details.

• To guide the learning, some questions like the following might help. Whenever possible, avoid asking questions that have simple yes or no answers. There's much less thinking involved with one-syllable responses because there's a 50% chance of being correct. Dig for some higher level thinking skills with open-ended questions like these.

<u>Where in the cup did you find the caterpillar?</u> (The answer will depend on the age of the caterpillar. Tiny ones usually stay closer to the bottom, the "teenagers" are all over the place, and the older caterpillars are usually found nearer the top.)

<u>How much silk did you find in the cup?</u> (Again, the age of the caterpillar will influence this answer. Younger, smaller caterpillars tend to keep the silk close to where they're eating. The older a caterpillar, the more likely it is that you'll find silk strands all over the inside of the cup.)

<u>What changes do you see in the frass?</u> (Size, color, and quantity all change as the caterpillar grows. Frass that's deposited by tiny caterpillars is small, light colored, and difficult to see. As the caterpillar grows, frass becomes large, dark green and very abundant.)

<u>What do you suppose are the black, fuzzy pieces you see on the bottom now and then?</u> (See page 35. As the caterpillar grows, it has to molt its old "shell" to get bigger and these pieces are the cast off shell. Each new size between a molt is called an instar.)

16   *Live* Butterfly Activity Book © 2002 Insect Lore

• You can come back to this activity over several days. The kids will quickly figure out what it is they're looking for and see the changes that have occurred. You'll even hear them proudly use the new terms they know to describe what it is they're seeing and drawing, too. Of course, you might want to become involved if someone uses the term "frass" inappropriately.

• Inside each 1-oz cup, it's easy to see the impact of living things on an environment. This tiny space has all that a caterpillar needs to become a butterfly and the environmental changes that the caterpillar causes should be readily apparent to the kids. You could discuss the fact that all living things impact their habitat and environment in both positive and negative ways; that this impact can occur on any scale from a 1-oz cup to an entire planet; and that the size of the organism (from micro to macro) is immaterial as to the possible extent of its environmental impact.

The word "habitat" is in quotes in the title of this activity because the cup isn't a true habitat for the caterpillar. It's generally accepted that a habitat is the area (or a *type* of environment) in which a living thing normally exists or where it's most likely to be found. Not too many Painted Lady caterpillars are normally found in 1-oz cups.

• To add to your list of concerns, you'll need to keep an eye out for unauthorized ants, rodents and cats around your caterpillars and eventually your butterflies. Entire populations of caterpillars and butterflies have been known to disappear overnight due to any of these three, not-so-sneaky predators. Plan accordingly!

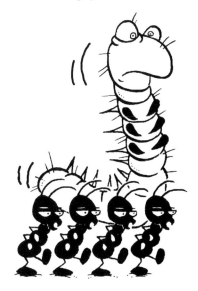

Micro-"Habitats"

Lesson Hints

• Sometimes using models or pictures can make things easier for you and the kids. Unfortunately, there can be drawbacks, too. For example, kids can lose a sense of how tiny a real butterfly egg is when they hold a marble-sized model. On the other hand, at least they can see what a real one looks like even if it is huge. Also, carefully choose the pictures you use so they convey the information you want the kids to get. You may want to teach one point but they're getting entirely another. No sense confusing the hooks you're using for all this new information.

• To better see the silk that's on the walls of the cup, hold the cup between you and a light source and slowly rotate the cup. You'll see what look like tiny cracks in the plastic reflecting the light. These are actually the silk fibers that the caterpillar has spread around inside the cup so it can climb on the slick plastic. A caterpillar has 2 spinnerets near its mouth that discharge a sticky thread that dries into a tough, silk strand that can be used like a ladder to get around its habitat. With a little luck and a cooperative caterpillar, you can see the spinnerets.

• The student sheet on page 90 can be used in conjunction with this activity as well as with Eating Machines on page 19. Some of the changes that the students are asked to look for in the cup are described on page 15.

Word Power

These are a few of the words and topics (hooks) you might want to have handy and use during this activity. Doing this could help keep everyone using the same hooks as the discoveries unfold.

data

frass

instar

molt

silk

spinneret

Painted lady caterpillars have one purpose in life and a very short time in which to fulfill it. The creature that's hardly visible at birth has about two weeks to eat its way through huge quantities of a specific food to attain the size it's required to be . It's a weight-gain program gone awry!

Content, Skills and Indicators—

1. characteristics of organisms, behavior, growth

2. measuring, comparing/contrasting, graphing

3. observing living things, effects of time and temperature

Pavilion School Kit Materials—

- Individual caterpillar in a cup for each student

<u>You provide:</u>
- Opportunities to observe
- Student Journal page from this book (see page 90)
- Hand-held magnifiers (optional)
- Drawing/writing materials (optional)

Other Insect Lore Butterfly Kits—

<u>Butterfly Garden</u>

With five caterpillars in each cup, the consumption of food and the buildup of silk and frass will be evident almost immediately. At the outset, individual growth is easily seen but as time passes, it becomes challenging to see size changes of specific caterpillars in the cup.

<u>Butterfly Pavilion</u>

As above, the activity in both cups is equally evident. While you may be tempted to open the cups for a better look, you risk more environmental destruction on the caterpillars than it's worth. Removing the lids on these cups is <u>not</u> a good idea.

TIMELINE:
This can be a 5-minute observation each day for about two weeks or until the caterpillar attaches itself to the lid.

PREP NOTES:
1. The timeline for the phenomenal growth you'll witness is based on the temperature. Cooler temperatures slow it down; warmer ones speed it up.

2. Caterpillars like to eat in the dark but the light in your room won't slow them down at all.

EATING MACHINES

THE IDEA   It will be easy for the kids to be aware of the incredible growth that a caterpillar undergoes: it's right in front of them. Odds are you won't expect them to measure their caterpillar to the nearest tenth of an inch and that's good. You can, however, use a variety of ways to help the kids track the growth. Check out LESSON HINTS for some ideas on measuring growth without violating the sanctity of the cup. On the other hand, there are some very interesting out-of-the-cup activities you can do with the kids using the extra caterpillars that came with your Pavilion School Kit. See COLD-BLOODED REACTIONS on page 23 and MOVE TOWARD THE LIGHT on page 27 for details.

THE METHOD

1. The food on the bottom of the cup is about an inch in diameter. Look at the suggestions below to get an idea of where you're headed.

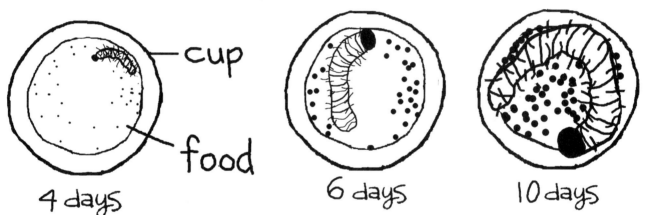

4 days   6 days   10 days

2. One of the most important parts of science is collecting data for others to study later. Help the kids understand that they should do their best and if your students are able to write, encourage them to try hard.

3. You're asking them to make a subjective guess about the length of the caterpillar compared to the size of the food on which it's crawling. At first, some serious "guided results" may be in order to help them see that relationship. The first pictures drawn on the student page will show short caterpillars but even with less help from you, the kids should see that the caterpillars get longer as times passes.

4. You'll want to add the date to each circle so the passage of time is noted, too. Basically, you're helping the kids gather data for what could be the first time for some of them.

         Live Butterfly Activity Book © 2002 Insect Lore

• Have the kids imagine what it might be like to be a caterpillar and have to eat *all* the time. That would mean some big changes in the way they live. Have them think about eating the same food all the time during every minute of every day, too. While that sounds yucky to people, it's very important for the caterpillar because without the right kind of food, the caterpillar could not grow and would soon die. For some species (like Monarch caterpillars) that's only one kind of plant, too.

If a human baby ate and grew at the same rate as some caterpillars, the child would weigh almost **6 tons** in only two weeks.

• To help them get a better idea about the size of the caterpillar compared to the food disk <u>without</u> removing the lid on their cup, you could use some of your extra caterpillars from the Pavilion School Kit. While the caterpillars are small and not too much silk has been spread in the cup, you can take the lid off one of of the extra cups to give the kids a better view. That way they can look down from the top and get a more accurate picture of what's happening in their own cup without disturbing it.

In the wild, Painted Lady caterpillars have to eat and grow fast for 2 reasons: (1) bigger is usually safer, and (2) its host plant growth cycle is fast. Most weeds do all their living in a short, fast season and the caterpillars need to match it or die.

• While moving the caterpillars to the 1-oz cups after they arrived (see page 3), you may have noticed that it wasn't easy to move them either onto or off of the brush. The 3 pairs of true legs at the front of the caterpillar have tiny hooks (called tarsi [*tár-sy*]) that help them hold onto silk fibers or the bristles of a brush. On the bottom of each of the 5 pairs of false legs at the middle and rear, you'll also find hooks (called crochets) that grasp the silk (or bristles) underneath. These hooks and the silk thread give the caterpillar firm footing on the leaf it's eating so its jaw is always close to the food. In addition, wind and predators (and maybe even you) have a hard time removing it from its place.

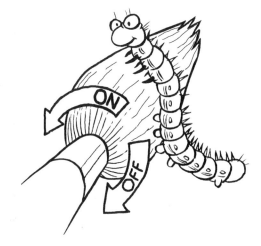

EATING MACHINES

Some scientists suggest that the powerful jaws of a caterpillar never stop chewing even if the caterpillar is resting.

• An amazing fact of butterfly life is that all of the nutrients it needs to survive as an adult are gathered as a caterpillar! That's right, all the exoskeleton-building nutrients that it needs to emerge, fly, and mate were consumed in the crawling stage of its life. As an adult, it feeds on nectar and minerals strictly to keep up its energy (see SWEET TREATS on page 63).

• You can draw a half-inch long vertical line on the outside of the cup to help track changes in caterpillar length. The kids make a daily comparison between the constant length of the line and the increasing length of the caterpillar.

• You can also help older kids monitor the consumption of the nutrient and the growth of the caterpillar. Use a permanent marker to draw a line on the outside of the cup at the starting level of the food. The kids can watch the level of food slowly drop as the caterpillar eats it and grows.

• If you have access to a digital or Polaroid® camera, a series of simple photos can dramatically show the changes that occur inside the small cup. Of course, digital pictures can then be emailed to any electronic location so others (like parents) can keep up with the fun.

WORD POWER

These are a few of the words and topics (hooks) you might want to have handy and use during this activity. Doing this could help keep everyone using the same hooks as the discoveries unfold.

    compare / comparison

    crochets

    tarsi [tár-sy]

Cold-Blooded Reactions

As you might expect, caterpillars are cold blooded, i.e. their body temperature changes with that of the environment around them. That sounds like a tough way to live until you realize that there are several good reasons for it. Well, they're good reasons if you happen to be a caterpillar.

Content, Skills and Indicators—

1. evidence, variables, response to environment
2. measuring, comparing, investigating
3. conclusions, natural processes, time and temperature
4. observe

Pavilion School Kit Materials—

- 2-4 extra caterpillars in 1-oz cups

You provide:

- Opportunities to observe
- Consistently warm location (ideally 73° to 78° F)
- Consistently cool location (ideally 65° to 70° F)
- Two small, identical boxes for the caterpillar cups
- Hand-held magnifiers (optional)
- Two simple thermometers (optional)

Other Insect Lore Butterfly Kits—

Butterfly Garden

With 5 caterpillars in a single cup, it's difficult to test and then compare the influence of temperature differences on their growth. You may want to skip this activity.

Butterfly Pavilion

You might test how temperature affects growth by keeping one cup cool and the other one warm. The differences could be dramatic and you'll have butterflies over a longer period since the cooler caterpillars will be slower to develop.

TIMELINE:
This activity may need 3 or 4 days to see some obvious differences.

PREP NOTES:
1. It's sometimes difficult to maintain constant temperatures if you're using the corners of your classroom as suggested in the text.

2. If you can find them, two thermometers will help you monitor the differences between the temperatures.

3. It may be better to use the extra caterpillars in the Pavilion School Kit instead of the ones the kids are watching. It's a judgment based on your knowledge of your class.

4. The caterpillars you put in the cooler area will be slower to develop into butterflies and the ones that are warmer will develop sooner. Plan for the timing difference as they go into the chrysalis.

COLD-BLOODED REACTIONS

THE IDEA

The fact that the vast majority of living things in the animal kingdom are cold blooded is often lost on the dominant species of planet Earth. People tend to think that the human way is the best (ergo, the *only*) way to live. Fortunately (or unfortunately, depending on your point of view) there are billions of creatures who not only survive in spite of their cold-blooded existence but prosper very nicely, thank you. Nature has given caterpillars an instinctive understanding that timing is everything. Their survival depends on appearing when the host plant on which they feed is vigorously growing. Most green plants grow best when it's warm and sunny; and that's when the caterpillars show up. You and this activity can help the kids make that connection.

THE METHOD

It may help to know that Insect Lore groups caterpillars that have hatched only minutes apart. That means you can be sure that they started life at about the same time. Growth will be fairly consistent among all the caterpillars in a single School Kit.

1. If you can, use an even number of caterpillars for each test group. Pick caterpillars that are at about the same point in their development and ones that you've had for about a week. Divide the number of cups you use in half.

2. Your biggest challenge may be having consistently warm and cool temperatures for the test groups. Some teachers have found that it's often warmer near the ceiling and cooler close to the floor in their classroom. There are some options as well as some cautions so check out the LESSON HINTS section for more ideas to consider.

3. When you've selected your warm and cool spots (see page 26 for the warning on <u>ants</u>), place a group of caterpillars in one box and label it "warm." Put the other group in a matching box and label it "cool." If you're using them, put a thermometer with each box and set the boxes in their respective locations.

4. If the difference between the temperatures is dramatic, say 5 to 7 degrees, the difference in the development of the two groups of caterpillars may be as much as 3-8 days. Even a 3- or 4-degree temperature difference, however, will account for an obvious difference in the development of the caterpillars. In any case, keep in mind that the caterpillars are headed toward becoming butterflies so you may want to get them back to the group after a week or so of separation. Just remember that the "cool" caterpillars will need longer to complete their growth.

THE METHOD

The actual temperatures that stop growth altogether are about 50°F or less on the cool side and 110°F or more on the warm side (OK, *hot* side). As you might expect, the ideal for caterpillars *and* plants is about 85°F.

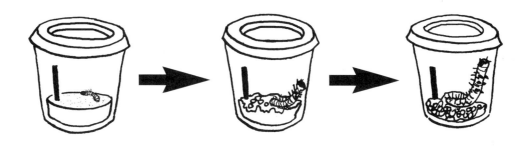

• With this experience, you're presenting a very important aspect of science activities and experiments in general. That is, of course, the importance of <u>variables</u>. To the best of your ability, you've tried to keep everything identical in this test *except* the temperature in which the caterpillars are living. The temperature is the <u>one</u> thing that's different. It's the <u>one</u> variable that you're testing to see how it *might* affect the growth of the caterpillars. The containers, the food, the water, the level of development of the caterpillars, the available light, the time you allowed, the alignment of the planets (just kidding), and everything else is the same. The <u>one</u> factor that's *not* the same is the temperature. So assuming you've controlled everything else, if there's a difference in the growth of the caterpillars, you can say without a doubt that temperature was the factor that caused that difference. Now, your job is to help the kids see and understand the concept of variables. When a scientist does an experiment, she controls all the variables but one at a time. That way, she can explain the outcome in terms of the influence of that one, particular variable. Then, she controls that variable and tests another one.

LESSON HINTS

COLD-BLOODED REACTIONS

LESSON HINTS

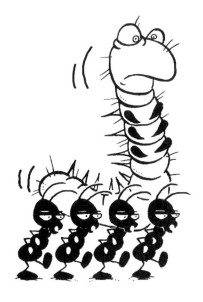

• There are ways to find other consistently warm and cool locations for the cups. Some of your colleagues may have extra cool or extra warm classrooms or you may have such rooms at home; lights may provide added heat (monitor the temperature closely inside the box); outside temperatures may be just right (i.e. no less than 55˚F); the school kitchen may have both temperatures within a few steps of each other; your custodian might know the perfect places in your building like near a water heater. Of course, there's a lot to be said for keeping it simple and maintaining control over your caterpillars, too..

• To add to the challenge, you'll need to keep an eye out for ants, rodents, and cats around your caterpillars that may be in far flung locations. Entire populations of caterpillars have been known to disappear overnight due to any one of these three predators. Maybe you ought to have a lesson about food chains ready just in case.

• A simple but effective mounting for the thermometers is classroom clay. Make sure the material doesn't touch either the bulb or the glass of the thermometer itself, however.

WORD POWER

These are a few of the words and topics (hooks) you might want to have handy and use during this activity. Doing this could help keep everyone using the same hooks as the discoveries unfold.

cold blooded

instinct

survival

temperature

thermometer

variables

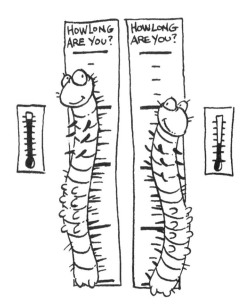

> *Painted Lady caterpillars are usually found in the top area of their host plant and often at the very outside edge of the leaf they're eating. Maybe they learned this behavior at caterpillar school or just maybe Nature has included this as a part of the instinct package all of them have at the start.*

Content, Skills and Indicators—

1. simple questions and investigations, survival

2. observing, hypothesizing, following directions

3. cause and effect, describe outcomes, natural world

4. compare, classify, measure

Pavilion School Kit Materials—

- 2-3 extra, week-old caterpillars

You provide:
- 1-2 twigs from bushes, kabob skewers, or chop sticks
- A flashlight or other bright, hand-held light source
- As dark a room as you can manage
- A gentle touch
- Other optional items (see the LESSON HINTS section)

Other Insect Lore Butterfly Kits—

Butterfly Garden

The single cup set-up of the Garden is best left unopened. You'll want to skip this activity.

Butterfly Pavilion

Even the two-cup option of the Pavilion is best left closed. With these 8-oz cups, you don't want to risk tearing the paper liner under the lid. It's *very* important for later development so skipping this activity is the better choice.

TIMELINE:
You should be using caterpillars that are 7 to 10 days old. You'll need about 15 minutes for the activity itself.

PREP NOTES:
1. When you remove the lid from a 1-oz cup to get a week-old caterpillar, you'll find silk everywhere. Take the caterpillar but leave the silk inside.

2. Be sure your subject caterpillars are active and not in the middle of a molt. You're OK if they're eating or moving in the cup.

3. if your kids are old enough, they could do all the tests in this activity. You'll just have to plan for the materials you'll need.

MOVE TOWARD THE LIGHT

THE IDEA

One of the most important things scientists do is ask questions. To get answers, they think up experiments and then share the results with anyone who'll listen. In the activity COLD BLOODED RESPONSES on page 23, you explored the effect of temperature on growing caterpillars. This activity aims to answer the questions; How do caterpillars respond to light and gravity? and, Which is the stronger influence? Caterpillars are often seen in the tops of plants and eating at the outside edges of the leaves. Who told them that's where the best leaves would be? How do they know? OK, so maybe there's lots more than one question. Help your class understand that's how a scientist thinks and that they're actually being a scientist when they ask a question that needs an experiment to get an answer.

THE METHOD

1. Just before the activity, you'll want to remove the caterpillars from their cups and place the caterpillars in a shallow dish on the inverted lid from their cup. Use the paint brush transport system to make the transfer. See LESSON HINTS for a refresher.

2. For the first of this three-part activity, you may want to dim the room but there's no need to darken it, yet. Of course, be certain that all the kids can see the action that's about to take place on the stick in your hands.

Facing

3. When you're ready, use the paint brush method to move the most active caterpillar from the lid to the middle of your twig, kabob skewer, or chop stick. Hold the stick vertically with the caterpillar head-down so everyone can see it.

4. The caterpillar will usually turn around and head up the stick. When it reaches the top, gently reverse the stick so the caterpillar is head down at the bottom. It may pause or hesitate but then it will turn around and go back the other way toward what is now the top.

THE METHOD

The surface of the twig, skewer, or chop stick is rough enough for the caterpillar to grasp without needing silk. A pencil or the paint brush handle may be too slick.

5. Repeat this reversal 2 or 3 times so everyone can see that the caterpillar prefers going upward (against gravity). If you have time and interest, give the same test to the other caterpillars to make sure the first one wasn't unusual.

6. If possible, darken the room further. Now, hold the stick horizontally with the caterpillar in the center. Use the light source and shine light at the head of the caterpillar.

The two remaining parts of this three-part activity might be more effective if you can darken the room as much as possible. At least dramatically reduce the amount of light in the room so the light you're holding is the brightest the caterpillar sees. Of course, the age of your students may make a difference as to how dark you can actually get it. See the LESSON HINTS section for more ideas.

MOVE TOWARD THE LIGHT

THE METHOD

7. When the caterpillar gets close to the light, you can either: (1) turn off the light, move it to the other end of the stick, and turn it on again, or (2) carefully flip the stick around so the caterpillar is now far from the light. In either case, after a pause or two, the caterpillar should begin to crawl toward the light. Repeat this test 2 or 3 times and try it with the other caterpillars as well if you wish.

(1)   (2)

8. The last part of this activity tries to determine which influence (gravity or light) is stronger for a caterpillar. In your darkened room, hold the stick vertically again but put the light <u>below</u> the stick pointing the beam up at the downward-facing caterpillar. This time, the caterpillar crawls downward. When it gets to the bottom, turn the light off, keep the light below the stick, flip only the stick around, and turn on the light again. The caterpillar may hesitate briefly at the top before it turns and crawls down to the light. Repeat this test as before.

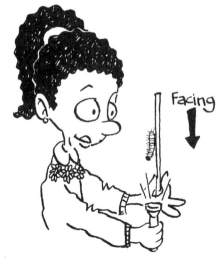

30

• This is a refresher on "the paint brush transport system." Hold the brush nearly perpendicular to the body with the bristles under the head. Then, gently roll the brush so the top side of the bristles rotates away from the front of the caterpillar. The caterpillar's front legs will grab the rotating bristles and it will be safely drawn onto the brush. To remove the caterpillar, roll the brush so the bottom side of the bristles rotates away from the front of the caterpillar. The tail and false legs will grab the surface first and the caterpillar will be safely moved.

• So, what's with the gravity and light activities? It was probably intriguing to watch the caterpillar tirelessly reverse directions each time you changed the up/down orientation of the stick or the location of the light in the first two parts of the activity. Then you might have been really surprised when it went *down* toward the light in the third part. That should tell you that caterpillars are more influenced by light than by gravity. Help the kids make the connection between the facts that (a) the youngest, most edible leaves are usually those growing on the outside edges of a plant facing the sun, and that (b) they're usually up and toward the light. So, the caterpillar has figured out that "food is near that bright thing somewhere" or something like that. Besides, if the caterpillar falls from the leaf on which it's dining, it has that overwhelming urge to go against gravity to get back to the dinner table.

• The responses you saw in the caterpillars are involuntary and, as you might expect, are triggered by light and gravity. Responses by an organism to stimuli such as light, gravity, water, heat, etc. are called tropisms [*tróe-piz-ums*]. Moving toward light is called positive phototropism; moving away is negative phototropism. Moving downward with gravity is positive geotropism. The caterpillar, however, displayed negative

MOVE TOWARD THE LIGHT

LESSON HINTS

geotropism as it moved against gravity involuntarily. But as you saw, the power of light was stronger than the pull of gravity for the caterpillar. The positive phototropic response is more powerful than the negative geotropic response in your caterpillars. They will always move toward the light. And you thought they were just dumb bugs!

• Like many others in this book, this is an activity where you may want to have the kids do the holding and the moving. You know them best and, thinking of caterpillar survival, only you can decide how much, if any, contact you trust the kids to have with live caterpillars outside of the cups. The grade, your facility and the darkened room may figure prominently into your equation but those concerns only lead to the suggestions that follow.

• If your kids are capable (and you have the interest and/or time), you might consider testing more variables. How could you test the stick preferences of the caterpillar? They might crawl better and faster on different kinds of surfaces. What behavior changes might you see if you use several light locations at once? How much real effect does the room light (ambient) have on the caterpillar's responses? What other kinds of lighting might make for interesting tests? You could try: ultraviolet (UV or black lights), colored lights (through colored gels or filters), low-watt bulbs (low lumen output), or even a hand-held florescent light source. So much science, so little time!

WORD POWER

These are a few of the words and topics (hooks) you might want to have handy and use during this activity. Doing this could help keep everyone using the same hooks as the discoveries unfold.

gravity

involuntary

response

tropisms [*tróe-piz-ums*]

How would it be? It'd be great if all you had to do was eat, rest, and be lazy all day and every night. You'd crawl around a little bit and change your clothes five times just because Mother said you had to. Of course, you'd live for only three weeks or so. Maybe it's not such a great life after all.

Content, Skills and Indicators—

1. change, behavior, structural functions

2. communicating, investigating, inferring

3. environments, living things, using senses

4. compare, observe

Pavilion School Kit Materials—

- Individual caterpillar in a cup for each student
- Several extra caterpillars and cups if needed

You provide:

- Opportunities to observe
- Hand-held magnifiers (optional)
- Drawing/writing materials (optional)
- Microscope (optional)

Other Insect Lore Butterfly Kits—

Butterfly Garden

If you're interested in pointing out a molted skin to the kids, you'll probably have to find it ahead of time. They're sometimes hard to locate in the pile of growing debris and frass in the cup.

Butterfly Pavilion

Since you have 2 cups, you've doubled your chances of easily finding a molted skin and halved the time you have to spend for all the kids to observe it.

TIMELINE:
As the caterpillars age, there's more to see so you might want to have lengthening observation times as they grow. Of course, the attention span of your kids may influence the amount of time you can give more than anything else.

PREP NOTES:
1. Each caterpillar is on its own schedule. If one seems more or less advanced than the rest, it's <u>not</u> because of a student even though a few might think so. You could revisit how variables are involved if someone is upset about the "lack of progress" a caterpillar is making.

2. This activity lends itself very nicely to some art and story and descriptive writing opportunities. See the LESSON HINTS section.

3. To see it more easily, you might want to retrieve a molted skin or two from the extra caterpillars you have with the Pavilion School Kit. A microscope would be really great, too.

THE LAZY LIFE?

THE IDEA   If the caterpillars are on track and everything is about normal, they're almost 10 days old, a little over an inch long, and are dark colored with a yellow stripe down each side. The kids can talk about them easily and use some new words correctly to describe them, too. This activity pulls together elements of previous activities and reinforces some ideas to help the kids get ready for the final instar and the change to the chrysalis. After that, the caterpillar is history and a whole new character takes the stage: a new Painted Lady butterfly!

THE METHOD   1. You could use the student sheet found on page 88 again (from CATERPILLAR ID on page 7) to help the kids review what they see inside the cup. You could look for any or all of the following parts labeled on their work:

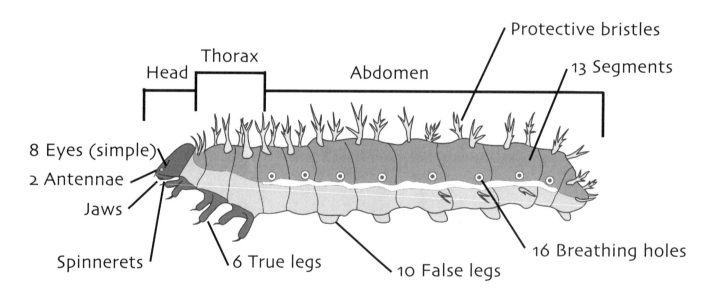

2. If you make a transparent copy of the student sheet for an overhead projector and work as a class, you can double check that the kids know what each part does by talking about each one as you label it and they look at it on their own caterpillar in the 1-oz cup.

3. By now it's obvious that the caterpillar has been eating a lot of food for its size. If you marked a line on the cup (see page 22), the level of the food will be well below it. Sometimes a willing caterpillar positions itself just right so a student can watch it eat. Use the pedestal idea from page 8 to help you get a better view of the munching.

THE METHOD

4. If the kids have had regular opportunities to watch the caterpillars, there will be times when no movement was seen in the cup. In spite of appearances, being a caterpillar involves huge changes and a great deal of effort so even they need to rest from time to time. There's no outward indication that a caterpillar is resting other than it doesn't move for several minutes at a time.

What you expect will no doubt be influenced by the kids' age and what you want them to know. For example, it's fine that pre-K kids know the silk comes from places near the caterpillar's mouth. A second or third grader might be expected to know that it comes from 2 spinnerets (see page 38). Older kids should be able to point them out on the caterpillar or on the drawing they made.

5. Another reason a caterpillar may not be moving or eating is that it could be preparing to molt. A caterpillar's soft body is inside a rigid case called an exoskeleton which doesn't grow. To get bigger, a caterpillar has to shed the old, smaller exoskeleton and then grow into the larger version of itself. One reason for so much silk in the middle of the cup is that sometimes the caterpillar will surround itself with silk for protection while molting. When the caterpillar is ready, the old exoskeleton splits along the back, opens, and the caterpillar peels it off—bristles and all. The caterpillar will molt 5 times and you can sometimes find the molted exoskeleton as a black, fuzzy ball on the bottom of the cup.

THE LAZY LIFE?

LESSON HINTS

• The point you'll want to make with this activity is that a caterpillar certainly <u>doesn't</u> have a lazy life. There are huge changes going on inside its little body right now that are only a fraction of the total change that's about to happen.

• With a review activity such as this, there are a variety of ways to make sure the kids have a grasp of what you've been doing for 2 weeks. Books, bulletin boards, games, and puzzles are just a few options. Have the kids write or suggest to you a story that compares a caterpillar to themselves including similarities and differences in how they move, eat, sleep, see , grow, etc. Adding pictures would go a long way toward improving the story, too.

• There are a variety of other support activities for younger grades that are appropriate but outside the scope of this book. You can check out these resources for more great ideas:

Echols, Jean (1997), *Hide a Butterfly*, A GEMS Guide, Lawrence Hall of Science, UC-Berkeley, Berkeley, CA

Graves, Kimberlee (1998), *Primary Theme Series: Bugs*, Creative Teaching Press, Cypress, CA

Shackelford, Karen (1994), *Bunches of Bugs*, LastingLessons, Dallas, TX

Sterling, Mary Ellen (1999), *Thematic Unit: Butterflies*, Teacher Created Materials, Westminster, CA

VanCleave, Janice (1999), *Play and Find Out About Bugs*, John Wiley & Sons, New York, NY

Watson, Jody and Penny Shafer (2001), *Butterfly! Flutterby!*, [self-published], Bakersfield, CA

• Of course, you're invited to contact Insect Lore directly to obtain any and all of the above titles and lots more!

> *Well, you've done it! You've nurtured over 33 caterpillars and a bunch of excited kids to the last step of a caterpillar becoming a butterfly. There are about to be some truly extraordinary changes that will take place in the 1-oz cups. It sort of makes you wish that butterflies could live longer.*

Content, Skills and Indicators—

1. life cycles, change, form and function

2. observing, comparing / contrasting

3. natural processes, description and discussion

Pavilion School Kit Materials—

- Individual caterpillar for each student
- 3 extra caterpillars and cups
- Pavilion for the chrysalids

You provide:

- Opportunities to observe
- A safe place to put the cups for chrysalis formation
- Hand-held magnifiers (optional)
- Drawing/writing materials (optional)

Other Insect Lore Butterfly Kits—

Butterfly Garden

When all of the caterpillars have become chrysalids, remove the lid and carefully peel off the paper liner. Some silk may be snagging on the chrysalids so trim any excess and tape the paper liner to the inside back wall of the Garden about 4 inches above the floor of the box next to the door.

Butterfly Pavilion

Watch for your 10 caterpillars to become chrysalids. Use the same cautions as above and tape the liners to the inside wall of the Pavilion about 4 inches above its floor. For insurance, you can sandwich the fabric between 2-inch pieces of tape. Use two hands to press the pieces of tape together firmly.

TIMELINE:
By now, the kids might use up 15 minutes per observation. Since the caterpillars are full-sized now, there's a lot to see until the chrysalis forms.

PREP NOTES:
1. Timing is everything now. Once the caterpillars form their J-shapes, they can't be disturbed until the chrysalis is complete. They're vulnerable at this stage of growth.

2. You can expect that when one starts to change, all of them will within a few minutes or hours of each other. It's as though there's a cosmic connection between them all.

3. Remember that if you slowed down or sped up development when you did COLD-BLOODED REACTIONS on page 23, then those caterpillars will be truly out of sync with the rest.

THE LAST LAP

THE IDEA Up to now the kids have seen the caterpillar grow from a tiny piece of life on a soft green pad to a fat, bristling chunk in the middle of a mess. While that's indeed a big change, the next step in the metamorphosis is even more amazing. This activity deals with several important aspects in the life of a mature caterpillar: the great quantity of silk it makes, some ways it defends itself, and of course, the amazing chrysalis. It's important to stress that when the caterpillar is in a J-shape and before the chrysalis is complete, it's very vulnerable. If it's carelessly handled or jostled excessively at this point in its life, the development to a butterfly may never occur. It'd be too bad for it to have come this far and not make it because it was shaken or dropped on the floor.

THE METHOD

It's difficult to show the kids but you might be able to see this behavior using one of the extra caterpillars in the Pavilion School Kit. Use a toothpick and carefully remove the silk from around the caterpillar. Gently poke it to disturb it and watch as it spreads silk under its feet to get away from the problem.

1. As the kids look into the cup, it's easy to see that the silk threads have been placed everywhere inside. To see them better, hold the cup about 10 inches from your face between your eyes and a dim light source. As you rotate the cup, the silk looks like tiny cracks all over the inside of the plastic cup. The silk is everywhere because it was used as a ladder for the caterpillar as it moved about inside.

2. The silk comes from 2 spinnerets which are tiny bumps or pegs located just below and a little under the mouth. You can tell the caterpillar is putting silk under itself when you see its head move from side to side as it walks forward. In addition, a lot of silk is a camouflage technique that helps mask the caterpillar's shape. The caterpillar also uses silk to draw the edges of leaves together for protection against predators and weather.

3. The dual purpose bristles (setae) are another "caterpillar image disrupter." A close look at them reveals that they come out in all directions along the 13 segments of the caterpillar's body. They're white or clear and have even smaller black-tipped branches that come out from the main stems. One purpose for the bristles is to make the caterpillar a hard-to-swallow meal for a predator. Another purpose is to blur the caterpillar's shape and make it less visible to predators when it's hiding inside the silk.

4. The caterpillar's tough exoskeleton is also a defense against some predators who might not be able to break it open. The caterpillar also likes to feed at night which means its dark-colored body is a plus. There's another interesting defense the caterpillar has but the only time it can use it is after it has become a chrysalis (see page 42).

5. The chrysalis (or pupa) stage of life is where the incredible change from caterpillar to butterfly occurs. To become a chrysalis, the caterpillar climbs on silk threads to the underside of the lid and finds a good place. Eating and moving have stopped and when it's ready, the caterpillar uses its spinnerets to spin a tight silk circle on the lid (called a cremaster [*creh-más-ter*]), grabs it with its 2 rear false feet, and hangs down head first in a J-shape.

THE METHOD

In the safety of the cup, about all the caterpillar has to worry about is being squashed by giant fingers. But it doesn't know that and Nature has provided some interesting defenses against predators. It might be easier to use the pedestal idea on page 8 to see the caterpillar.

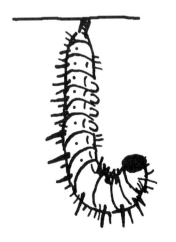

THE METHOD

This is a very exposed time for the caterpillar because it can't move around as before and to go from the J-shape to the protective chrysalis can take a full day.

In the wild, the pupal stage may last for weeks or months if it's too cold to continue.

6. During this next process, it appears that the caterpillar is just peeling off its fuzzy skin from the exoskeleton underneath. Actually, the skin along the back of the caterpillar splits and the wet, soft, greenish chrysalis wiggles its way out of the old caterpillar skin. Sometimes the newly shed skin doesn't drop off completely and remains attached by a single thread to one end of the chrysalis. It hangs next to the chrysalis like a little black powder puff that will never be used.

7. In 2 or 3 hours, the chrysalis shortens, hardens, and takes on a golden hue. (See page 45 for more details.) As you might expect, development within the chrysalis is temperature sensitive. Around 74°F the change is complete in about 7 days. But, drop it to the mid-60's and it can be as long as 12 days. When the chrysalids are 1 day old, the extra ones could be used to test this sensitivity but you'll need to attach them to paper strips first.

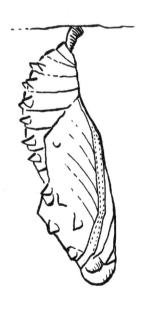

8. Whether or not you're going to test temperature sensitivity, you have to secure the chrysalids in an appropriate way. Of course, within a few hours of each other, the bulk of the chrysalids will just go into the Pavilion. To do this, wait a day for a chrysalis to harden completely and then carefully remove the lid from a 1-oz cup. You may have to gently remove or even trim any silk threads that are clinging to the chrysalis. Attach the lid on the inside of the Pavilion fabric wall using a 2-inch piece of clear tape with the chrysalis facing the inside. All the lids will fit on the wall in 2 or 3 rows and about an inch apart around the entire inside circumference of the Pavilion. Keep the rows 4 to 8 inches above the floor of the Pavilion. If you're into insurance, stick a piece of tape on the outside of the Pavilion against the one on the inside.

9. To test the temperature sensitivity of the chrysalids, you'll need two separate, pint-sized, wide-mouth containers. Tape a lid and chrysalis combination from the extra cups to the bottom 2 inches of an 8x2-inch piece of paper towel. Make five more of these set ups and then place three strips into each container with the chrysalids inside and the excess towel draped over the rim. Cover each container with a piece of paper towel and hold it in place with a rubber band. Trim any excess paper towel. Time to test a variable! Use those warm and cool spots you found earlier (see page 26) to lengthen or shorten the pupa stage.

THE METHOD

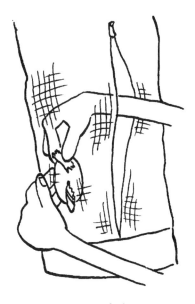

This is one of those times when you have to make a judgment call. You can mount all the chrysalids yourself and be sure it's done quickly and correctly or let the kids have a role in it somehow and just expect it to take a little longer.

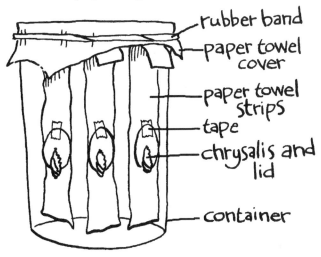

rubber band
paper towel cover
paper towel strips
tape
chrysalis and lid
container

THE LAST LAP

LESSON HINTS

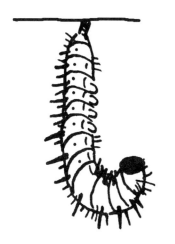

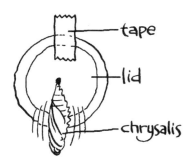

tape

lid

chrysalis

• When the caterpillar first hangs head down in the J-shape and the chrysalis hasn't emerged, it's very easy to see all the legs (both true and false legs), segments (there are 13), bristles (with their tiny branches) and breathing holes (spiracles) which are clearly outlined with white circles. It's the best opportunity to see so much detail on a motionless caterpillar.

• Sometimes you may open a cup and find the chrysalis has fallen from the lid. Not to worry! Gently place it on a piece of paper towel on the floor of the Pavilion and it'll be fine. You may have several there by the time you're finished.

• There's not much a chrysalis can do to defend itself but it's likely you'll see it do so many times. When it feels threatened because it's been touched or bumped, the chrysalis flexes some abdominal muscles and it begins to shake or vibrate rapidly back and forth. The intent is to scare away a predator with sudden movements. In addition, the grayish color of the chrysalis helps it to blend in with the surrounding shadows.

• What looks like a quiet waiting time is actually a period of astounding changes inside the chrysalis. Four large, beautiful wings develop; the false legs disappear; a jaw becomes a straw; simple eyes become large, compound, and able to see color in all directions; long antennae grow; and much more. Some of these changes can be seen on the outside as the chrysalis gets older, too. The eyes, wings, antennae [an-tén-knee], breathing holes, and abdomen may be visible before the new butterfly emerges.

WORD POWER

These are a few of the words and topics (hooks) you might want to have handy and use during this activity. Doing this could help keep everyone using the same hooks as the discoveries unfold.

antennae [an-tén-knee]

camouflage

cremaster

metamorphosis

predator

pupa [péw-pah]

You could be in the middle of the most important lesson or test of the year but if the butterflies decide to emerge at that moment, you might as well forget it. Even if it's only one in five or ten or thirty-five, it will captivate everyone—including you! So be prepared for the arrival in your room.

Content, Skills and Indicators—

1. life cycles, inherited characteristics, changes

2. observing, comparing / contrasting

3. living things, natural processes, differences

Pavilion School Kit Materials—

- Pavilion with live butterflies and chrysalids

You provide:

- Opportunities to be amazed
- A table or reading light for better viewing (optional)

Other Insect Lore Butterfly Kits—

Butterfly Garden

It may be a challenge to get everyone around the Garden all at once to view an emergence. You'll have to employ some creativity so everyone can see into it clearly. Some extra lighting might help.

Butterfly Pavilion

You'll have a fairly easy time getting everyone to see into the Pavilion. There are almost no bad seats. Some extra lighting would help visibility here, too.

TIMELINE:
Each emergence lasts a few seconds but the interest lasts much longer. Allow a full 10 minutes for each group to watch the new butterfly.

PREP NOTES:
1. There's more about this in the text on page 46 but be ready for the bright red blotches that are a normal part of each new butterfly's start. It's a red liquid that's not blood but still very important to the butterfly. Be sure the kids are expecting it because it can be a big surprise otherwise.

2. An emergence doesn't take very long so don't miss the action by thinking you can take your time getting to it.

"They're here!"

The Idea

An emerging butterfly has crumpled, wet wings. Your first reaction may be that you've failed as a grower. Not true! Be patient and be amazed with the entire process.

The most important part of this activity is timing. However, luck has as much to do with it as anything. It seems that no matter how carefully you plan it, the butterflies frequently emerge (they don't really "hatch") when either you're not ready or not there to see it. But even if you and the kids get to see only one make its appearance, it's very exciting. Hopefully, with more than one to emerge, you'll be able to witness one or several of the big moments. As mentioned earlier, even if you're in the middle of something important and the butterflies begin to emerge, you might as well join in because the kids will be completely gone.

The Method

Placing a small table or reading light next to the Pavilion so that it shines light inside will make it easier to see the butterfly as it moves about. It's also easier to track the changes occurring in the other chyrsalids. Keep in mind that chrysalids are heat sensitive and you may speed up the rate of emergence if you use a high intensity bulb. A regular bulb is just fine.

1. Sometimes the first emergence catches you a little off guard and you wonder how to be ready for the next one. Take a close look at the remaining chrysalids. You might notice that some of them have undergone what seems to be a color change. They look much darker than they did earlier. In reality, the material covering the chrysalis has become thinner and more transparent as the time for emergence approaches. It's possible to clearly see the dark colors of the wings and even some features within the still closed chrysalis. This usually happens anywhere from 12 to 24 hours prior to emergence.

2. The colors on the chrysalis are often truly extraordinary. There are shades of gold, silver, and copper as well as green, orange, white, and sometimes a pearly white. As you slowly rotate a chrysalis in the light, these colors become very apparent and they can be breathtaking. Of course as the chrysalis ages, these tend to fade.

3. The tiny golden cones or pegs on the chrysalis run down the back of the butterfly inside. The locations of the antennae and eyes are very apparent on the opposite side of the chrysalis. When it opens, the chrysalis splits along this "mask" and the butterfly wiggles out head first.

THE METHOD

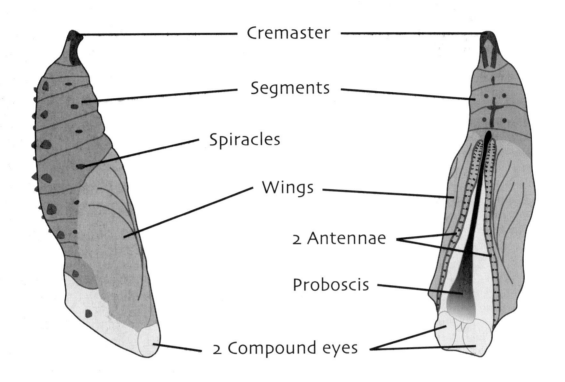

Cremaster

Segments

Spiracles

Wings

2 Antennae

Proboscis

2 Compound eyes

4. Upon emerging (they don't hatch), a butterfly's immediate response to the world is to go against gravity (see page 31). Instinctively it knows to struggle upward and since it can't yet fly, it has to walk. By contracting a series of muscles, the butterfly pumps blood (called hemolymph) into the crumpled wings. It even hangs upside down to let gravity help get them ready for flight and to speed up the nearly 2 hour drying and filling process. Once the wings are rigid, the butterfly draws all the blood out and seals the tubes. That leaves a strong, light-weight tubular scaffolding inside to support the wing and eliminates blood loss if a wing gets broken.

Sometimes Nature throws a genetic curve ball and there's an obvious deformity of some kind. It could be poorly formed wings, a missing leg, a proboscis that fails to work properly, or some other variation from the norm. It may test your teaching skills to help the kids realize that this is a natural part of all life. In some cases, you may opt to remove the butterfly in question; in others, it may survive just fine.

"They're here!"

LESSON HINTS

• Aside from the emergence itself, one of the most dramatic things you'll see is the butterfly suddenly excrete a large quantity of a dark, red-colored liquid that looks exactly like blood. It's true that butterflies have blood but it's usually colorless since it doesn't carry oxygen. This red fluid is called meconium [*meh-kóe-knee-um*] and it's possible you saw some spots of it when you had chrysalids forming. It's a watery material that has a red pigment in it and is a by-product of the dramatic physical change from caterpillar to butterfly. And this change is not equal. The caterpillar has much more body mass than the butterfly and this physical difference becomes meconium. During the wing-filling process, the butterfly excretes most of the meconium in big drops and it flows down the side of the Pavilion. It can also make red splotches on the fabric and the bottom of the Pavilion. While it is harmless to the butterfly and quite a normal process, it can be very unsightly and, to the uninformed, appear to be the evidence for butterfly-grower brutality. It does wash out of the Pavilion, though, so go ahead and enjoy the show while you have your butterflies. Just be sure to tell the kids about it ahead of time!

Don't wash your Pavilion until all the butterflies have emerged and literally flown the coop. Then just use a little warm, soapy water and hand wash and rinse it. Let it air-dry completely before storing it or using it again.

• It's possible that having your caterpillars and/or chrysalids mature at different times might increase your chances of actually watching more butterflies emerge. If you placed either caterpillars or chrysalids in a cool area to slow down their growth (see pages 25 and 41), they'll be that much further behind the development of the others. Perhaps you can time it so that you and the kids can watch a complete emergence after all. Remember, if you want to push it along, you can warm it up a little. Science is so fun and life science is so amazing!

WORD POWER

These are a few of the words and topics (hooks) you might want to have handy and use during this activity. Doing this could help keep everyone using the same hooks as the discoveries unfold.

emerge / emergence

meconium [*meh-kóe-knee-um*]

When you stop to think about it, the transition from a rather homely critter like a caterpillar to the captivating grace of a butterfly is rather astonishing. The body parts on the butterfly are so radically different from those on the caterpillar that it's difficult to fathom the extent of all the changes.

Content, Skills and Indicators—

1. characteristics, form and function, inquiry

2. observing, communicating, inferring

3. using senses and simple lab tools

Pavilion School Kit Materials—

- Butterfly Pavilion School Kit and 33 butterflies

You provide:

- Opportunities to observe
- Student Journal page from this book (see page 92)
- Hand-held magnifiers (optional)
- Drawing/writing materials (optional)
- A table or reading light for better viewing (optional)

Other Insect Lore Butterfly Kits—

Butterfly Garden

The butterflies in your Garden are ideally suited to this activity. Just be careful since you have only 5 of them, however.

Butterfly Pavilion

The 10 butterflies in your Pavilion are ideally suited to this activity as well. Careful handling is also a god idea.

TIMELINE:

You can have butterflies to watch for as long as 3 weeks but you may want to release them after about 10 days. Allow several minutes each for observation and for the kids to make notes and pictures or to talk with you about their discoveries.

PREP NOTES:

1. You want the kids to be comfortable using correct terminology to describe what they see in the Pavilion.

2. It's easier to see the parts of a living butterfly if you sprinkle the sugar water "nectar" you feed them on flowers. See page 48.

3. You don't have to throw away a dead butterfly. They are amazing creatures to observe with a lens. See pages 12 and 51 for more ideas.

4. Some people are not willing to touch, or pick up, an insect, even a butterfly. You might want to give the class a heads-up and find out who might need to just watch.

THE BUTTERFLY'S TURN

THE IDEA   For 2 or 3 weeks you and the kids have focused on the life and characteristics of a Painted Lady caterpillar. That bit of life has undergone an astounding transformation and you have been gifted with a new Painted Lady butterfly. It seems impossible that 2 creatures that appear to be so radically different from each other are in fact one in the same life form. It could be science fiction except that you watched it happen. This activity will help the kids become familiar with their new butterfly and give them an idea about what they're looking at and what to call it. You may or may not want to use the Journal page found on page 94.

THE METHOD

After emerging, butterflies don't need to eat for about 24 hours. It's best to have food ready for them, however.

1. With 33 or so butterflies in one Pavilion, you'll need to make sure they have food available all the time. There are several options for feeding them, too. For all of the options, the basic nectar recipe is a rounded teaspoon of sugar in a half-cup of water.

1 tsp sugar / ½ cup water

A cotton wick or several cotton balls in a dish soaked with the homemade nectar can work, too.

- The easiest method may be to place a folded paper towel in a shallow dish on the bottom of the Pavilion and soak it daily with the nectar. It does get messy with so many butterflies eating in one place. You'll want to use a clean towel every 2 or 3 days and two dishes is a good idea.

THE METHOD

- The most aesthetic feeding method is more trouble but very pleasing to watch. Yellow carnations, mums, daisys, or other simple flowers can be placed in water in a small, heavy container on the floor of the Pavilion. Use a pipette to sprinkle the nectar on them once or twice a day and watch the butterflies "feed" on the flowers.

- The simplest feeding system may be to use wedges of fresh oranges each day. Wedge a medium orange and use the knife to pulp the center of the wedge. Squeeze it slightly to collect the juice in the center and put the wedge on a small dish in the Pavilion. Sometimes small pieces of watermelon can be used. Score the surface with a knife so juice will collect in the grooves and place the pieces on a dish in the Pavilion.

Contrary to folk myth, a butterfly can still fly even with the loss of some of the scales on its wings. What you want to avoid is breaking a wing so please, handle with care. They don't grow back!

2. To get a closer view of a butterfly, you may expect the kids to be able to pick up one correctly and look at it. To begin with, they need clean, <u>dry</u> hands. Use the thumb and index finger of the writing hand to gently grasp a resting butterfly (the wings are closed over its back) by its wings just above the body and as close to the shoulders as possible (see #1). Let go if you get only one pair of wings or are too far from the shoulders to avoid extra flapping which may damage the wings. Only a very light pressure is needed. If the butterfly seems agitated or over-excited, hold it with its legs up and it will calm quickly (see #2).

(1)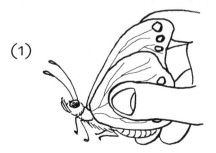

(2)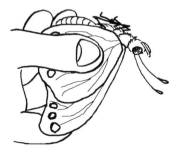

THE BUTTERFLY'S TURN

THE METHOD

The wingspan of a Painted Lady butterfly is a little over 2 inches. The butterflies in these illustrations are larger so it's easier to see what the label is showing.

3. While you may not expect anatomical and/or verbal perfection from your class, it's certainly OK to expect them to be able to describe a butterfly using accurate terms. These illustrations can guide you as you help the kids connect names to the parts they see on their butterflies. Using top and bottom views might help things a little, too.

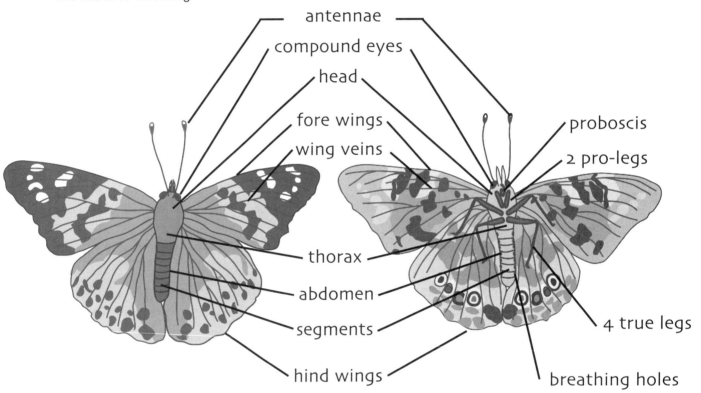

antennae
compound eyes
head
fore wings
wing veins
proboscis
2 pro-legs
thorax
abdomen
segments
4 true legs
hind wings
breathing holes

LESSON HINTS

• In case there was some question, Painted Lady butterflies are insects (see THE ARTISTS' MODEL on page 53) and they really do have 6 legs. *Really!* The two back pairs are readily visible but the pro legs (prothoracic legs) are folded tightly under the head and thorax. They're modified for touching a leaf during the egg-laying process; for touching flowers before eating to find nectar; and for cleaning the front portion of the head and body.

Live Butterfly Activity Book © 2002 Insect Lore

• Butterflies are always on a liquid diet. The proboscis responds to a nectar stimulation, uncoils (see SWEET TREATS on page 63), and the butterfly draws the liquid food inside. A tiny straw is sandwiched between 2 blood vessels that are normally empty and coiled up under the head. To feed, the butterfly forces blood into the 2 tubes and the proboscis uncoils as they fill. Food can then be taken from deep inside a flower through the long straw between the blood-filled tubes. To retract the proboscis, the butterfly draws the blood out of the tubes and it coils back into place. A party noise maker can model this action but you're using air instead of a liquid to make it work. Close enough.

• By now younger kids are probably quite good at using a hand lens as well as other simple lab tools. If you'd like a review, however, check page 11 for the finer points of hand lens operation.

• Some people are hesitant to look at a dead butterfly. While the loss may be regrettable, it gives you and the the kids a great opportunity to see details that are normally just a blur in the Pavilion. For example, the compound eyes are truly remarkable when seen closely. Each facet (and there are over 10,000) has a fine, hair-like projection that gives the eye a generally fuzzy appearance from a distance. Other details are the segments and tips of the antennae, the tiny claws (tarsi) on the ends of the legs, the amazing arrangement of the scales on the wings and body, and so much more. Take advantage of the incredible views found on a dea— OK, a *non-living* butterfly.

THE BUTTERFLY'S TURN

LESSON HINTS

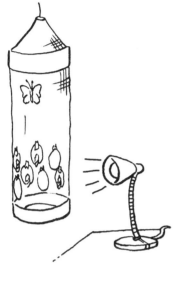

• By now you've seen just how much meconium can be released when you have 33 butterflies in one compact place, especially a white one. They're not very thoughtful, either, and will release it any place they happen to be standing. It's not unsanitary or unhealthy, it's just unsightly. In fact, other than a fine layer of light-colored scale dust that covers the surfaces in the Pavilion over a few days, there's nothing you can see or have to deal with in terms of "cleaning the kennel." Butterflies are clean and quiet and probably the easiest pets you'll ever have in your room.

• The Pavilion should hang in a bright, sunny location when it's full of butterflies. They're definitely sun worshippers and enjoy the warmth and the light. You do want to avoid drafts, however, so placing the Pavilion under or near an air duct isn't a good idea. If the location you have to use is an inside corner or other cool, dark spot, consider using a table or reading light so you can both see the butterflies better and appease their light-loving nature. They're really low maintenance and this isn't a lot to ask in return for all the pleasure they provide you. Now, is it?! And speaking of pleasure . . .

• If you keep the butterflies more than 3 days, you can expect them to mate. If this presents a problem for you, then you'll have to deal with it by releasing them before they mature. The butterflies are not concerned with human sensibilities and are driven to continue their species. It's natural and wonderful and you can count on seeing the courting and mating behaviors (see LIFE GOES ON on page 75) in butterflies that are from 3 days to about a week old.

WORD POWER

These are a few of the words and topics (hooks) you might want to have handy and use during this activity. Doing this could help keep everyone using the same hooks as the discoveries unfold.

proboscis [*pro-bóss-iss*]   pro-legs
compound eyes   true legs
fore wings
hind wings
wing veins

As you look at the Mona Lisa in the Louvre in Paris, you have to marvel at the fact that Leonardo was, for the most part, self-taught. He began by looking at and drawing what he saw in Nature, too. Perhaps there's a budding da Vinci in your class that will use this activity to make a statement!

Content, Skills and Indicators—

1. simple tools, communicate, form and function

2. classifying, comparing / contrasting

3. awareness of living things, better descriptions

4. count, observe

Pavilion School Kit Materials—

- Butterfly Pavilion School Kit and 35 butterflies

You provide:

- Opportunities to observe
- One toothpick (at least for you if not the whole class)
- Drawing/writing materials
- Hand-held magnifiers (optional)

Other Insect Lore Butterfly Kits—

Butterfly Garden

The butterflies in your Garden are ideally suited to this activity. Just be careful since you have only 5 of them to work with, however.

Butterfly Pavilion

The 10 butterflies in your Pavilion are ideally suited to this activity as well. Careful handling is also a good idea here.

TIMELINE:
This activity could last 30 minutes or more with older kids if you really get into it.

PREP NOTES:
1. This activity has its roots in the idea that everyone will know the characteristics that make an animal an insect. That should be where you start and where you end.

2. Some people are not willing to touch, or pick up, an insect, even a butterfly. You might want to give the class a heads-up and find out who might need to just watch.

THE ARTISTS' MODEL

THE IDEA   No doubt your experience in front of kids has told you that there are huge differences in the ways people learn and how they express what they've learned. The single greatest challenge for a teacher is probably trying to find ways to accommodate these differences to cause learning to occur. You may want to review pages vi to viii for some ideas on dealing with this concern before getting into this activity. You might be surprised by some of the pictures you get from doing this activity. After all, observing and drawing Nature is how Leonardo da Vinci began his career.

THE METHOD   1. A review of what you did on page 5 in the activity HOMES IN A CLASSROOM might help get some brains in the groove you want for this effort.

2. To do this correctly, you might want the kids to pick up a live butterfly (see page 49 for the "how to") and carefully look at it. Then again, your class may be too young or too something for this strategy. It's better to see the real thing so even a dead butterfly is preferable to a picture.

The outcome you're seeking is to make sure the kids are as certain of the fact that a spider is *not* an insect as they are that a whale is *not* a fish.

3. As they're looking at the butterfly, talk about the insect they're seeing. Keeping in mind the learning model on page viii, include the following in what you say:

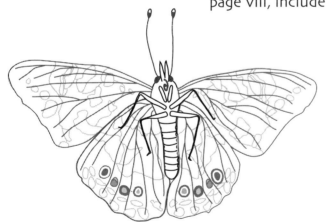

- Insects have 6 legs. Some of the kids will argue that they see only 4 but you already know about the pro legs (see page 50). On the butterfly you're holding, use the toothpick to gently extend them away from the body just below the head. They look like brushes and butterflies with pro legs like this are sometimes called brush-footed butterflies. They're modified for touching a leaf to identify it during egg-laying; for touching flowers in the search to find nectar; and for cleaning the front portion of the head and body. But they're still legs and with the other 4, that makes 6.

- <u>Insects have 3 body parts.</u> The eyes, antennae, proboscis, and palpi ([*pál-pee*] the pair of stubby projections between the eyes) are on the head; the wings and legs are attached to the thorax; and the spiracles are in the segments along the sides of the abdomen.

- When it has them, <u>an insect has 4 wings.</u> What may look like just 2 big wings on the Painted Lady butterfly are actually 4. There are 2 fore wings and 2 hind wings. An interesting feature is that there are more tubes (see page 45) along the leading edge of the fore wings than along the trailing edge of the hind wing. This allows the wing to curve downward and create lift during flight.

Wings can break and they don't grow back so be careful! However, if you manage to remove some colored scales, the butterfly can still fly when you release it. Yes, that's right, they can still fly even after losing scales but not if they have broken wings.

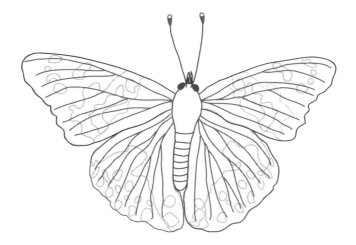

- <u>Insects have 2 antennae.</u> The antennae on the Painted Lady are like those found on most butterflies: they're smooth, segmented, have knobs on the end, and are used for touching and smelling.

- <u>Insects have 2 eyes.</u> Outside of the wings, the eyes may be the most prominent feature of your butterfly. They are compound eyes which are made up of thousands of individual facets that may have tiny, hair-like projections between them. These eyes are excellent, too. They see movement easily, give the butterfly a wide field of view, and can distinguish a variety of colors very well.

THE ARTISTS' MODEL

THE METHOD

This 3-step drawing is also found on the student sheet on page 93. The idea is to draw a basic butterfly in essentially 3 easy steps and then add more details later.

4. Now that you've explored a little bit, consider having the kids make a simple but accurate drawing of their Painted Lady butterfly. These steps might be useful for you to follow. Tell the kids this first drawing is what they'd see looking down on top of the butterfly.

- Start with a small, horizontal egg-shape. This is the head and you can add eyes, antennae, and palpi now if you wanted to stress their location on the head. By the way, you can't see the proboscis in a top view.

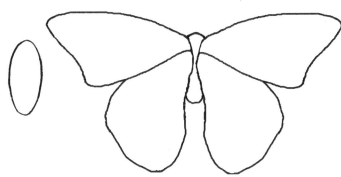

- In your drawing, the thorax is a narrow but elongated oval that extends vertically from the head, but it's about twice the length of the head. Since this is the top view, you'll be adding the 4 wings. The shape of the wings can be an important feature that identifies a butterfly species so use some care when drawing an outline.

- The abdomen the is longest of the three body parts and can be an oval that's drawn about double the length of the thorax. You might add segments to the abdomen. Remember this drawing is for general purposes and probably won't be submitted to the Louvre just yet. At this point, you're looking for general awareness more than anatomical precision.

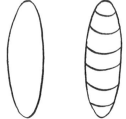

5. The bottom view uses the same proportions for the head, thorax, and abdomen but adds other features.

• Draw the head and eyes again and add the palpi and antennae between the eyes. This time you can add a curled-up proboscis, too.

• Toward the middle of the thorax, draw 2 segmented legs on each side. The pro legs can be added as just a pair of lines to the upper half toward the head. The 4 wings can be drawn in the background attached to the thorax.

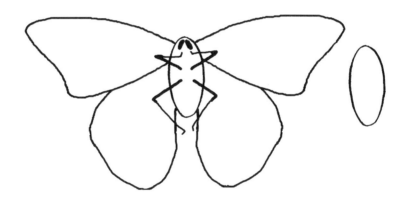

• The same proportions used for the top view can be used for the bottom view of the abdomen. Drawing segments with spiracles on the sides are easy additions.

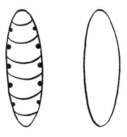

The Artists' Model

Lesson Hints

The intensity of the colors varies from season to season. They seem to be more intense if cooler temperatures during the butterfly's development keep it inside the chrysalis a little longer.

"When a butterfly flutters by, it's the flash of colors that'll catch your eye."

Butterflies bring out the poet in almost everyone.

Word Power

• There's a beautiful arrangement of colored scales on your Painted Lady butterflies. Looking from above, both fore wings and hind wings are generally orange with large areas of brown closer to the body. The fore wings are about one-third black at the outer tips with 5 white spots in the black. The orangy-pink "rouge" for which the Painted Lady was named is found on the underside of each fore wing at mid-wing near the leading edge. The hind wings are mostly orange with brown and black spots toward the edges. On each hind wing, 4 of these black spots have blue centers and faint yellow outlines. From underneath, you'll see designs of white, brown, tan, black, blue, and purple and the 4 small, black eyespots along the trailing edge of the hind wings that are unique to *Vanessa cardui L.* The kids can color both sides of the butterfly outlined on the student sheet on page 94.

• Some of the kids may want to try to convince you that a butterfly has fur on it. Actually, only mammals have true fur for a body covering. The body of a butterfly is completely covered with colored scales. Depending on their location, the scales are modified for particular purposes. There are scales on both sides of the wings and they're arranged neatly in rows that overlap each other. This improves the air flow over them and keeps them from being easily dislodged. If you gently scrap them from both sides of a piece of wing, you'll find they're attached to a clear membrane that's stretched between the empty veins in the wing.

• Colors and wing designs are more than decorations for the butterfly and inspiration for humans. Butterflies see colors and patterns in the ultraviolet range of light and the main purpose is to be able to identify mates within its species. Colors and patterns also frighten or fool predators and can provide some camouflage, especially if the wings are closed.

Here's a word (hook) you might want to have handy and use during this activity. Doing this could help keep everyone using the same hooks as the discoveries unfold.

palpi [*pál-pee*]

> *In the short-term it seems like most insects and crawling critters have no purpose in life other than to make things difficult for humans. In the grand scheme, however, they have vital roles in the quality of life on Earth for all living things. OK, but you still might say "Gross!" for some of them.*

Content, Skills and Indicators—

1. characteristics, form and function, inherited traits

2. classifying, comparing / contrasting

3. awareness of living things

Pavilion School Kit Materials—

- Butterfly Pavilion School Kit and 35 butterflies

You provide:

- Opportunities to observe
- Hand-held magnifiers (optional)
- Drawing/writing materials (optional)

Other Insect Lore Butterfly Kits—

Butterfly Garden

The 5 butterflies in your Garden might appreciate a break. Use them as living references any time, however.

Butterfly Pavilion

There are 10 butterflies in your Pavilion that would be happy to answer any questions about some of the unusual members of their class (if they could).

TIMELINE:
This 20-minute lesson can be extended to several days by using bulletin board displays, student reports, and field trips in the neighborhood.

PREP NOTES:

1. You might find a local person who knows a lot about insects and is willing to share some experiences with your class.

2. It's easy to get distracted by the many bizarre critters found in the huge phylum of animals called "Arthropoda" (see page 83). That's OK as long as you focus mostly on the class "Insecta." They're strange enough on their own!

3. There's a wealth of information about "bugs" available from the web, government agencies, colleges and universities, museums, libraries, local experts, and commercial outlets. There's no shortage of material to look at and consider.

JUST BAD PRESS?

THE IDEA   Swatting a mosquito is a reflex. Everyone knows ants don't belong in a kitchen. Butterflies are beautiful and harmless. Call an exterminator if you see cockroaches or termites! Bees make honey but they sting you. It seems most of the billions of insects in the world have had some pretty ugly press over the years. However, take people out of the equation and many of the "bad" insects suddenly fit perfectly into the scheme and balance of Nature. With this activity you'll help the kids think about and maybe reconsider what the view from the top of the food chain should be regarding those "yucky" creeping and crawling things of planet Earth "down there" at the other end.

THE METHOD   1. To get the kids thinking about "good" or "bad" insects, you're welcome to use the following stories. Of course, finding another one you like or, better yet, having the kids write their own are good options, too.

• While searching for food on a clear, sunny morning, 2 ants found a very large and very dead grasshopper. As one began the task of trying to move the huge grasshopper, the other ant followed a scent path and returned to the ant hill. There it relayed a message to the other ants that food was available. Following the same scent path they found the dead grasshopper and together, they moved or cut up the remains and took them back to the ant hill. Those grasshopper remains fed the ant colony for many days. The cycle continued as what had been the grasshopper now became soil nutrients that supported new plant growth the following Spring. The new plants were a food source for many animals including new grasshoppers and more ants!

Live Butterfly Activity Book © 2002 Insect Lore

- A maple tree was killed by a disease that swept through a forest late one summer. In Spring, a termite queen found the dead tree and made it the home for her new colony. For a very long time the termites lived in the trunk of the maple tree eating the dead wood. A powerful storm blew the tree down but the termites stayed on inside. After a few years and many generations, the termites were gone and there was nothing left of the trunk but a soft mound of very rich soil exactly where the tree had been. Another strong storm in the Fall blew seeds of all kinds through the forest. Spinners from a maple tree landed on the mound. When Spring arrived, the spinners and seeds from many other plants started to grow quickly in the fertile soil.

2. You're setting up what could be a fascinating experience with a wide variety of insects. You could start with a simple list like lady bugs, ants, cockroaches, honey bees, termites, mosquitoes, grasshoppers, butterflies, dragon flies, house flies, praying mantids, etc. and have the kids extol the vices and virtues of each. Then go for some higher level thinking skills and have the kids consider how "good" or "bad" these same critters would be on a planet without any kind of human connection.

3. These stories are quite benign and far removed from the daily interaction of humans and insects. They do, however, illustrate some of the roles that ants and termites have in Nature that don't directly impact humans. Or do they? It's pretty obvious that along with some other organisms like bacteria and fungi, insects play a major role in the removal of dead plants and animals from the Earth. It's safe to say that without this insect behavior, the planet would be hip-deep in organic left-overs.

THE METHOD

You may want to start off by helping the kids understand that the notion of "good" or "bad" insects is a very subjective or personal decision. It's along the same lines as saying peas or snakes or storms are "good" or "bad."

Just Bad Press?

Lesson Hints

By the way it's true that butterflies are harmless (see The Idea on page 60); it's the *caterpillars* that can do the damage to trees and plants. Of course, Painted Lady caterpillars dine almost exclusively on weeds so you can feel good about working with them.

• If your kids are old enough, there's a lot to consider when it comes to careers involving bugs. The exterminator always comes to mind first, of course, but entomology (the domain of truly dedicated bug-lovers) has medical, agricultural, environmental, and global applications. A favorite term for the avid bug hunter is palentological entomology or, finding *really old* insects in rocks. Even as a hobby, insects are truly intriguing!

• The book <u>Bug Faces</u> [Murawski, Darlyne A. (2000), National Geographic Society, Washington D.C.] and many other good references (available from Insect Lore, naturally) can help you study the good, the bad, the fun, the misunderstood, and the really strange critters of the bug world.

• An excellent, PC-compatible CD, *Travels with My Ant Lion,* is available from Pat and Dr. Richard Kaae, Cal-Poly, Pomona, CA. For more information about this CD and other great insect resources (including some real eye-openers), contact them at:

Pat Kaae or weevilways@earthlink.net

PO Box 20000

San Bernardino, CA   92406

Be sure to tell them that Insect Lore sent you.

• As is the case with most things, it's not just the one or two insects that are a problem, it's the one or two *million* all at once that can wreak havoc! When you're dealing with an ant or cockroach infestation, their cosmic significance is totally lost when you believe that's about how many there are in your home.

Word Power

These are a few of the words and topics (hooks) you might want to have handy and use during this activity. Doing this could help keep everyone using the same hooks as the discoveries unfold.

entomology / entomologist

Like all living things, humans need food but lately, some have gone overboard on too much of a needful thing. Butterflies, on the other hand, can indulge in a high-sugar diet and not only get away with it but even flourish. Maybe it's all that courtship during their incredibly short, active life span.

Content, Skills and Indicators—

1. simple investigation, basic needs, behavior

2. following directions, controlling variables, inferring

3. living things, natural processes, collect information

4. compare, observe

Pavilion School Kit Materials—

- Butterfly Pavilion School Kit and 33+ butterflies

You provide:

- Cotton swabs for whomever will be testing the butterflies
- Small containers of nectar solutions (see text)
- Rinse water and paper towels for the inevitable
- Other simple items as called for in the text (optional)

Other Insect Lore Butterfly Kits—

Butterfly Garden

The butterflies in your Garden are ideally suited to this activity. Just be careful since you have only 5 of them to work with, however.

Butterfly Pavilion

The 10 butterflies in your Pavilion are ideally suited to this activity as well. Careful handling is also a good idea here.

TIMELINE:
Allow about 20 minutes for the basic testing so the kids (and the butterflies) aren't rushed.

PREP NOTES:

1. This activity requires some pretty good eye-hand coordination and fine motor control.

2. You'll want to be as set up as possible before the kids get involved. You may want to have containers of various nectars around the room for testing and that takes planning.

3. Have some paper towels and plain water handy for sticky fingers and spills. It'll happen.

4. It would probably be best to use butterflies that are a week old. That should give the kids and the butterflies a chance to get used to each other.

5. The results are more obvious if you keep the test butterflies away from nectar for 24 hours. You may have to isolate small groups to use for the various tests.

SWEET TREATS

THE IDEA

This activity has four interesting tests you can perform if you have the time and the kids have the understanding. They're fairly simple but some materials and set up are required for all of them. There's also more time needed to complete them so plan ahead.

Feeding time is an event that always attracts a crowd at a zoo or aquarium. It's as if merely feeding the animals is a sure sign that they're being well treated. There's no question that the butterflies in your care are being well treated (see page viii) but no matter how hard you try, their life span is only 2-3 weeks on a diet consisting of just one entreé: a sugar-water nectar. The tasting and eating (or, more correctly *drinking*) behaviors of a butterfly is what you'll see in this activity. And if you're so inclined, you could also discover the limits of the butterfly sweet tooth, whether they're attracted more by color or by nectar, and if you can get away with using an artificial sweetener on them.

THE METHOD

1. You want the test butterflies to be a little hungry. You can isolate the ones you'll be testing or simply remove the food from the Pavilion if you'll be using all the butterflies. In any case, a 24-hour period without nectar won't hurt the butterflies and will make the results more obvious.

2. The basic nectar recipe is 1 teaspoon of sugar dissolved in a half-cup of water or, like many nectars, about a 5% solution. If you're the only one doing the testing, you'll need one container and any small amount of nectar (e.g. 1 tablespoon) would be plenty. Have several cotton swabs and a toothpick or two along with the nectar for the tests.

1 tsp sugar / $\frac{1}{2}$ cup water

Paper towels and some plain rinse water within reach would be a good part of the set up, too.

3. Assuming you want the kids to get some hands-on time, you might want to place some small containers (e.g. 2 ounce cups) around the room with a tablespoon of the basic recipe in each one. Each container will also need the same number of cotton swabs as there will be butterflies being tested with the nectar from the container.

4. Place a cotton swab in the nectar and leave it in the cup for now. You'll be touching the swab to several places on the butterfly's body and looking for a reaction to the taste of the nectar. The behavior that indicates the butterfly is tasting will be the proboscis emerging and uncoiling.

The Method

5. Pick up one of your hungry butterflies and hold it upside down to keep it calm before doing the tests. If you need a refresher on how to pick up a butterfly, check page 49.

There has to be a comfort level for you concerning the kids' ability to hold a butterfly in one hand, a nectar-soaked cotton swab in the other, while conducting the test at the same time. For younger students, you'll probably be the one to show them how a Painted Lady butterfly tastes and drinks nectar.

6. Remove the cotton swab from the cup and flick off excess nectar. Gently but definitely touch various locations on the butterfly (see Step #7) with the tip of the soaked swab. Give the butterfly a few seconds to react. When the proboscis uncoils, the butterfly is responding to the taste of the nectar and is trying to locate it to eat. For now, remove the swab before it can drink so you can continue to test other locations on the hungry butterfly.

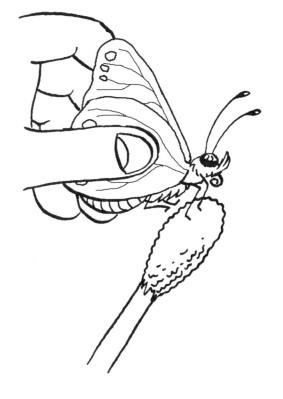

SWEET TREATS

You may want to use your non-writing hand to hold the butterfly since the cotton swab has to be targeted at tiny areas. You probably have better fine motor control with your writing hand.

7. Test these areas by touching each one with the tip of a nectar-soaked swab. Look for the butterfly's reaction.
   - both antennae (tips and stems)
   - tips of the palpi (between the eyes)
   - the proboscis (probably hidden slightly)
   - prolegs (may need to be teased out, see page 54)
   - the second pair of feet (tip of each leg)
   - the third pair of feet (tip of each leg)
   - each wing tip
   - tip of the abdomen
   - other places (e.g. leg joints, under the thorax, etc.)

LESSON HINTS

• The results of these tests should tell you that Painted Lady butterflies taste with their feet and the response is most evident on the tips of the second pair of feet, too. This makes sense because these feet are the first part of the butterfly to contact a flower and a possible nectar source. If nothing is tasted, the butterfly won't waste time uncoiling its proboscis (see page 51).

The Butterfly Sweet Tooth Do humans or butterflies detect different concentrations of "nectar" more readily? You'll need five 8-oz cups, water, sugar, cotton swabs, measuring cups, measuring spoons, and an eyedropper or pipette.

If you use 1 spoon to stir all the solutions, be sure to start with the lower concentrations and move to the higher as you stir to dissolve the sugar.

1. Start with a half-cup of basic nectar (see page 64) in one of the 5 cups. Pour a half-cup of plain water into each of the 4 remaining cups. Dissolve 2 teaspoons of sugar into one of the cups of plain water (about a 10% solution, see page 70). Next, dissolve a half-teaspoon of sugar into a second cup (a 2.5% solution). Finally, dissolve a fourth-teaspoon of sugar into a third cup (a 1% solution). Don't add sugar to the last cup. Make sure the kids don't know which concentration is which but mark the cups some way so *you* can keep track.

2. Test several hungry butterflies with each solution but this time, since you know the magic spot, touch just the second pair of feet with a swab. Be sure to use a separate swab for each solution and keep track of the butterfly's response to each solution.

3. Use the pipette to squirt a small amount (e.g. a fourth-teaspoon or less) of nectar into the mouth of each of your test humans. You'll want to rinse the pipette and have the kids swish with some plain water between test solutions. Have them describe or rank the sweetness of each solution in secret and then talk about the results after all the tests.

What you'll likely discover is that the kids were able to detect sweetness better than the butterflies. If the butterfly is going to risk stopping for food, then the nectar had better be worth it. There's predator danger and mating/egg-laying time lost when pausing at a flower The butterfly needs to find a good food source or it moves on to another. It turns out that humans can detect sweetness at levels as low as a 2% solution. That's about a teaspoon of sugar dissolved in 1 cup of water. Butterflies can't detect concentrations that are less than about 4% or greater than about 7%. They literally want to eat on the fly.

Colorful Fussiness   What are the favorite colors of the Painted Lady butterfly? You'll need some construction paper (black, yellow, white, blue, orange, pink, and red but *not* green) and scissors.

1. Remove all the materials from the floor of the Pavilion and line it with the black paper. Trim the paper to cover the bottom completely. If you want to test a smaller number of butterflies, then remove them from the Pavilion and place them in a test box. Make sure it's sunny inside of it. Line the bottom of the box with the black paper.

If you have them, several smaller containers made from shoe boxes with cellophane-covered windows and vent holes would give more kids the chance to watch the color-selection process.

SWEET TREATS

LESSON HINTS

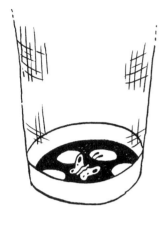

2. Cut a 2-inch circle from each of the remaining pieces of colored paper. Hang the Pavilion in a sunny location and arrange the colored circles on the black paper in the Pavilion. Spread them out as much as possible.

3. This is the observation part and may require as much as 10 minutes to establish a trend. Tell the kids to keep track of the colors that most of the butterflies are attracted to or investigate (i.e. quickly touch) most often.

4. Rearrange the colored circles and repeat the observation. You can do this as much as you think it's necessary. Once color preferences are determined, you could try different shapes of the favorite (squares, triangles, stars, etc.) to see if shape has an impact on the selection process, too.

The kids will most likely decide that Painted Lady butterflies prefer yellow or white followed by blue, orange, and pink. Red doesn't seem to be attractive and it's possibly not even seen by them. However, they have great color perception (see page 55). Green wasn't used this time because it's attractive for egg laying and a green, paper circle would be rejected for that purpose after the butterfly examined it. The shape test shows that a shape (even in the favorite color) has little influence on butterflies.

It's more manageable to test a few hungry butterflies than it is to use all 33 in the Pavilion but that means having to make smaller containers for the test group. See page 67 for an idea.

Good Taste in Colors Are hungry butterflies attracted more by nectar or color? You'll need 5 small vials or containers, water, sugar, food colors, and cotton balls.

1. Mix a batch of basic nectar (see page 64) and fill each vial or small container with it.

2. Use the food colors to tint the nectar in 4 of the containers to yellow, blue, red, and pink. One remains clear. Stuff cotton into all 5 containers so that it's completely colored and saturated and there's only a tiny bit of it sticking above the container. The cotton plug in the clear container will appear white and the others will be colored.

3. Arrange the 5 containers in your test area and observe the feeding behavior of the hungry butterflies. Rearrange the food containers a few times to test the results. You may have to use some other hungry "volunteers" for this test.

It was probably evident that the nectar was the attractive force in this test. Some butterflies may have even fed on the red cotton as well as on the other colors. There were probably more on the yellow and white containers, however. The next step in this test could be to use dry, empty containers with one of the colored circles attached to the neck of each container and a matching colored cotton plug stuffed in the neck. Fill only the red-collared container with red nectar, plug it with the red cotton, and repeat the test. That way, you'll clearly show that the nectar has a greater attractive influence than even a color that doesn't register on the butterfly radar screen or a dry "flower" that's the favorite color (yellow).

• As you consider doing these simple tests with younger students, it might be just as effective to have them hand feed the butterflies and forego the experimental aspects. Watching a butterfly feed right from their fingers is a wonderful experience that your kids will always remember and will probably do again.

• An excellent extension activity would be to use an artificial sweetener instead of sugar and repeat some of the tests. The kids will discover that a Painted Lady butterfly doesn't bother to count calories and won't confuse saccharin with sugar. It's considered a non-food source and the proboscis stays coiled.

SWEET TREATS

LESSON HINTS

Sweet-o-meter

.0247

• Of course as you conduct these tests, you and/or the kids will be moving the butterflies from place to place and you and/or the kids will no doubt let go of and/or release a butterfly prematurely and/or accidentally. It'll happen. It may be a trauma for some but if it's inside the classroom, you can just wait for a quieter time to recapture the escapee. If it's outside, bid them *bon voyage*! You could always have a small butterfly net handy for such occurrences, too. Just remember, it'll happen.

• An amazing fact of butterfly life is that the food it needs as an adult is for energy only! All the body-building nutrients that it needs for a *lifetime* were gathered as a caterpillar. That's right: the only reason a butterfly needs nectar is to maintain its energy level for the rigorous adult lifestyle it's living. Essentially, it's food strictly for sex and flying. How cool is that?

• For those who compute such things, here's how the percent of concentration was figured: a level teaspoon of white sugar weighs about 5.7 gm and 8 oz of tap water weighs about 230 gm. 5.7 ÷ 230 = .0247 or about 2.5%. Crude perhaps, but close enough for butterflies that prefer a 4% to 7% concentration.

• You're reminded about the note on page viii telling you that nothing you do with the butterflies should be detrimental to them. These simple tests you give the butterflies are short and interesting and when you're finished, let 'em eat! Keep in mind all those eyes watching you and the way you treat your lab animals. It's an on-going demonstration.

WORD POWER

These are a few of the words and topics (hooks) you might want to have handy and use during this activity. Doing this could help keep everyone using the same hooks as the discoveries unfold.

concentration

solution

dissolve

> *If it's daytime, that flitting creature in the yard is probably a butterfly. If it's nighttime and the porch light's on, then it's probably surrounded by moths. There have to be more differences between butterflies and moths than just their hours of operation. Here's your chance to end the confusion.*

Content, Skills and Indicators—

1. different structures, form and function, behaviors

2. inferring, hypothesizing, communicating

3. simple generalizations, living things, environment

4. compare, classify, observe

Pavilion School Kit Materials—

- Butterfly Pavilion School Kit and 35 butterflies

You provide:

- Opportunities to observe

- Hand-held magnifiers (optional)

- Drawing/writing materials (optional)

Other Insect Lore Butterfly Kits—

Butterfly Garden

The butterflies in your Garden are ideally suited to this activity. Just be careful since you have only 5 of them to work with, however.

Butterfly Pavilion

The 10 butterflies in your Pavilion are ideally suited to this activity as well. Careful handling is also a good idea here.

TIMELINE:

The basic lesson may need only 15 minutes but you'll need more for the observations (especially if you visit the web site suggested in LESSON HINTS).

PREP NOTES:

1. It's usually pretty easy to find dead moths to study. Look (or have someone *else* look) inside both indoor and outdoor light fixtures.

2. It's possible that a colleague will have some live silkworm moths to share (see LESSON HINTS).

3. Of course, if the season's right, you could try the old porch-light-and-sheet trick to gather your own sample of moths (see LESSON HINTS).

4. You might want to check local colleges, libraries, museums, universities, botanical gardens, etc. for butterfly and moth collections that you can bring to your classroom. Some places may even offer school presentations.

"WhaWuzZat?!"

THE IDEA

Some entomologists (those folks whose passion in life centers on insects) have estimated that there could be as many as *17,000* different species of butterflies in the world. They add that there could also be upwards of *11,000* species of moths worldwide. And these are just the <u>known</u> species!. There are nearly 800 species of butterflies found in North America alone so it's understandable that you can't keep track of the names of them all. But you can use this activity to help the kids know that the big whatever-it-was that just fluttered by was definitely a butterfly and not a moth. It's kind of like generally knowing the differences between insects and spiders (see pages 5 and 54).

THE METHOD

As soon as you say "all" or "every" there will be an exception (or ten) to the rule. You'll want to help the kids understand this basic principle of life. For example, there's a species of butterfly that spins a cocoon before entering the pupa stage. But the differences the kids discover with this activity will be those they'll find in nearly all butterflies and moths they study later.

1. This is a great opportunity to let the kids discover physical differences between butterflies and moths just by looking and talking with each other while not receiving too much input from you. It's the essence of *Explore* (see page viii).

2. Ideally, each student has living butterflies and moths to compare. Reality check: "it probably ain't gonna happen." You can, however, make sure they know the characteristics of a butterfly (see THE BUTTERFLY'S TURN on page 47) so they can readily identify the differences seen in a moth.

 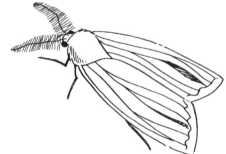

3. A simple diagram of a moth similar to what they did for a butterfly in THE ARTISTS' MODEL on page 56 might help. Moths are definitely insects but you're looking for some clear distinctions that set them apart from butterflies like:

   • moth antennae look like feathers;

   • a moth folds its wings flat over its body; and

   • moths have generally fatter "bodies" than butterflies.

4. You'll want to consider some behavioral similarities and dissimilarities between moths and butterflies, too.

- Both are insects and have all the traits of that class.

- Moths usually fly at night; butterflies like the daytime.

- A moth caterpillar wraps itself in silk (a cocoon) when becoming a pupa. (*Usually*) there's no such covering on a chrysalis.

- Both animals are drawn to pretty flowers for food and pollinate the plants they visit.

- Some of the caterpillars of either insect (more so for moths) can be damaging to food crops of humans.

- Moths rely more on scent chemicals (pheromones) to identify mates than butterflies who use colors.

- Butterflies are usually brightly colored while moths are often less visible (but some moths are gorgeous).

THE METHOD

Here's another one of those exceptions to the rule. There are some cousins in the butterfly family called skippers. They look like a cross between a butterfly and a moth because they're small, fuzzy, and quick but chunky and not too colorful. The telltale signs are antennae that look like tiny fish hooks and a flight pattern that resembles a flat stone skipping quickly across a pond, hence the name.

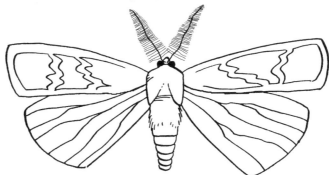

- Many teachers raise silkworm moths from eggs every year. You might find a colleague or a "friend of a friend" who has a batch they'd be willing to share with you and your kids. If mulberry leaves happen to be out of town for the winter, Insect Lore can provide you with silkworm "chow" that's as close to Nature as it can be short of being a real mulberry leaf. If you want your own silkworm eggs, caterpillars, and moths, take a look at the product "Silkworm City" from Insect Lore, too.

- Colors and wing designs are more than decorations for the butterfly and an inspiration for humans. Butterflies see colors and patterns in the ultraviolet range of light and the main purpose is, of course, to be able to identify a mate within its own species. Colors and patterns also frighten or fool predators and can provide some camouflage, especially if the wings are closed.

THE METHOD

"WHAWUZZAT?!"

LESSON HINTS

• If the weather is warm and you're so inclined, here's an easy way to collect moths for your class. It can be as simple as hanging an old, white tee-shirt on the wall behind a lighted porch light or as elaborate as spreading a white sheet in a funnel shape around a bright light in the back yard. Set up either one of these at night and be ready to see an amazing assortment of the local, 6-legged night life. Plan on your beacon attracting many more insects than just moths, too.

• So, if moths are nocturnal (prefer the nighttime), why do they fly toward lights? It's likely they're confusing lights with their historical direction finder, the moon and are responding to tropisms (see page 31) to fly upward and toward it. It must sometimes be a challenge for an urban moth to get anywhere.

• If the kids are capable, there's always the possibility of having <u>them</u> collect some moths and bring them to class. It could lead to a whole new level of awareness for everyone. It may be challenging to identify some of the denizens of your nighttime neighborhood but there is help available. A particularly well organized and color-photo documented web resource for you is *www.npwrc.usgs.gov/help/faq/bflymoth/idmoth.htm*. Count on spending some time there even after you answer your questions.

> *Your Painted Lady butterflies have a lifetime of living to cram into about three weeks. Of course they have only one purpose in life and they fulfill it with gusto. After just 2 or 3 days as a butterfly, both sexes are mature and mating can occur. It's a very quiet but a very obvious process.*

Content, Skills and Indicators—

1. simple investigations, life cycles, inherited characteristics

2. observing, following directions, inferring

3. natural processes, cause/effect, living things

4. count, compare, measure

Pavilion School Kit Materials—

- Butterfly Pavilion School Kit and 33 butterflies

You provide:

- Bouquets of fresh host-plant leaves (optional)
- Hand-held magnifiers (optional)

Other Insect Lore Butterfly Kits—

Butterfly Garden

The 5 butterflies in your Garden have only one thing to do as adults. Mating will occur frequently and you might expect to see some egg laying, too.

Butterfly Pavilion

The 10 butterflies in your Pavilion have the same drive to reproduce so look for courting and mating behaviors during the first week or so.

TIMELINE:
Depending on your class, you may skip this activity altogether, talk about it for a few minutes, or spend about 20 minutes observing the egg-laying process.

PREP NOTES:

1. If you keep the butterflies more than 3 days, expect to see courting and mating behaviors. You'll need to be ready to explain why they're stuck together end-to-end.

2. Sometimes it's a good thing to encourage egg-laying. Then again, if they hatch, you may have several *hundred* very hungry caterpillars on your hands. And no, they don't eat lollipops.

3. Raising butterflies is a great hobby. There are important things you'll need to know that go beyond the scope of this book, however. Some more research would be a really good idea!

LIFE GOES ON

THE IDEA It's important that you're prepared for the courting and mating behaviors of your Painted Lady butterflies and that you're able to answer the inevitable questions that will arise. The drive that powers this process is a profound force that's a part of every living thing on Earth and understanding that fact makes caring for local habitats as well as the global environment all the more significant. Whether your class is young enough to be satisfied with simple answers or old enough to raise a couple of generations of Painted Lady butterflies, the kids need a sense of the delicate balance of life on this planet. The information here is for you. You can share it with your class as you see fit.

THE METHOD 1. It takes 2-3 days for the reproductive organs to mature in a Painted Lady butterfly. The courting and mating rituals often begin late in the afternoon or early evening and can continue throughout the night. Apparently, timing is everything. Predators aren't as active at these times and it's usually the warmest part of the day, too.

2. At first glance, it may seem like there are no identifying differences between the males and females. Fortunately, the butterflies have it figured out and there are a few subtle signs you can point out to the kids. On average, females are larger than males, especially in the abdomen. Males are the ones flitting about the sides of a female in an attention-getting display of fluttering wings and colors.

Males are also the ones that curl their abdomens into a hook shape in an effort to clasp the female's abdomen. If he's successful and she allows it, the two are joined at the tips of their abdomens and are facing away from each other. The male grips the female with organs called "claspers" which are located at the tip of his abdomen. They're not pinchers but are used to hold on to the female during mating. Mating can last several hours and the grip is strong enough to allow a joined pair to fly together even while mating

3. Painted Lady butterflies will mate from 1 to 3 times within the first week or so of life as long as they're warm enough. Frequently, females will mate only once but males will continue to strut their stuff in an effort to find other females who are willing to be impressed.

THE METHOD

4. Within a few days and up to 2 weeks after mating, it's possible that your butterflies will lay eggs. With a little effort, you can improve both the chances and the quantity by helping the mother-to-be feel comfortable.

- It's helpful to isolate a mating pair in a smaller but sunny box that doesn't get hot. Make sure they have a supply of nectar (see page 48). Check page 49 (if necessary) for a review of how to move a butterfly, except this time, pick up both at once.

- Painted Lady butterflies prefer hollyhock, malva, nettle, and thistle leaves for egg laying but you can substitute radish, spinach, and romaine lettuce leaves with limited success. Soak the leaves you use for 2 minutes in a solution of a pint of water, 1 tablespoon of bleach, and a drop of liquid soap. Rinse them well and dry them completely. Put the stems in water in a small container and place this bouquet with a mating pair. Keep in mind that without the preferred host plant, the caterpillars may grow but becoming a butterfly may not happen.

In some species, males release a scent to entice the females to mate. This pheromone and the brilliant ultraviolet colors of his wings usually have the desired effect. The result can be an increase in the number of times that mating will occur, especially in an enclosed space.

LIFE GOES ON

THE METHOD

5. The egg-laying process is a fascinating ritual. The female follows a fairly rigid procedure before laying the first egg.

- She sees the leaf and flies to it (it's the right color).
- She lands on it with her feet (it tastes right).
- She touches it with her antennae (it has the right scent).
- She brushes it with her prolegs (it's the right feel).

After the first egg is deposited, she may shorten the testing process but will still make periodic checks of the leaf with her prolegs as she lays the rest of her eggs.

Process

See ▸ taste ▸ smell ▸ touch ▸ lay

LESSON HINTS

• Potentially, there could be lots of eggs to hatch. If you're inclined *not* to be a god-parent to a few hundred caterpillars, don't put leaves in the Pavilion. There's normally little egg laying without leaves present to receive them. Your best bet would be to have a Release Party before the eggs are deposited (see INTO THE GARDEN on page 79).

• If you do have lots of eggs, expect caterpillar casualties unless you have a steady supply of acceptable leaves and the time to maintain the feeding. The caterpillars will need daily feeding with fresh leaves and a means to form chrysalids when the time comes. This could be a great project to send home with the kids as long as they clearly understand the requirements.

WORD POWER

Here's a word (hook) you might want to have handy and use during this activity. Doing this could help keep everyone using the same hooks as the discoveries unfold.

pheromone [*fáir-uh-moan*]

It's time to make a very real and very positive contribution to your local environment. Of course this means releasing the butterflies. There are some plants and additions to gardens you can provide that will encourage them to stay in the neighborhood. It's kind of the ultimate culminating activity.

Content, Skills and Indicators—

1. environment, needs of living things, behavior

2. predicting, following directions, observing

3. natural world, living/non-living things, changes

4. count, compare

Pavilion School Kit Materials—

- Butterfly Pavilion School Kit and 33+ butterflies

You provide:

- An outdoor release location (optional)
- A camera (optional)
- Other interested people (optional)
- A butterfly-friendly garden space (optional)

Other Insect Lore Butterfly Kits—

Butterfly Garden

The butterflies in your Garden are usually happy to be a part of the release. Just be careful since you have only 5 of them to work with, however.

Butterfly Pavilion

The 10 butterflies in your Pavilion are probably willing to leave. Careful handling is also a good idea here.

TIMELINE:
The actual release can take from just a few minutes to an entire afternoon depending on what you want to teach.

PREP NOTES:
1. The biggest concern upon release is the weather. Warm (above 70°F) and sunny is the ideal forecast. Summer and early Fall are usually the best seasons for predictable warmth.

2. The next major concern at release time is the appetites of the local bird population. They may figure you're trying to feed them and are all to happy to help out.

3. Some people can become attached to the butterflies and are sad to see them fly away. It *is* a good thing, however, so they can take their place in Nature.

4. If you really plan ahead, you can have plants and garden features that supply butterflies both their food and host plant requirements.

INTO THE GARDEN

THE IDEA

It's possible that you can't (due to weather) or don't want to release the butterflies. Having them live their short lives in your good care is perfectly fine. Odds are they'll live longer inside than they will outside.

If you're planning to do this activity, then you're planning to improve the local environment. The Painted Lady butterflies you've raised and are about to release are an excellent addition to the neighborhood ecosystem and you can be sure that they'll remain there, too. Well, in one form or another, that is. They may quickly become part of the food web or survive long enough to lay eggs for a more lasting contribution. Whatever the outcome, you, the kids, and the butterflies will have improved your community in a variety of ways. Good for all of you!

THE METHOD

1. You can release butterflies at any time during their lives. The only major consideration is the weather, specifically, the temperature. If it's less than 55°F, they can't fly and will shiver or bask to achieve a flight muscle temperature of over 80°F. It's easy to see that butterflies are basically solar powered and both need and enjoy a warm sun. You could consider their wings as solar heat collectors.

2. On the appointed day, remove the food sources from the Pavilion and take out any remaining lids that are taped to the sides. The best release site is near a tree or large bush in the middle of a garden where the butterflies can land and hide from hungry birds.

Live Butterfly Activity Book © 2002 Insect Lore

3. There are 2 main ways to release the butterflies. One is easy; the other is more involved.

   • As you go outside, the butterflies will probably be drawn toward the sun. Orient the opening toward the sun then unzip the Pavilion all the way. Sometimes you might have to nudge them toward the openings and encourage them to fly.

   • Have each student pick up a butterfly and release it or hold onto it and release them all at once. While that sounds like a dramatic send-off (and it can be), there are timing and student age issues you have to consider.

THE METHOD

4. It's OK to be a little wistful about watching *your* butterflies strike out on their own. After all, you raised them for this very moment and now it's come and gone. Just remember, these are butterflies and you're helping them fulfill small but important destinies!

Of course, in your care what butterflies need (food) and want (a mate) has been always close at hand. They've also been protected from predation, bad weather, flying long distances, and accidents. A release may be more important for you than for your butterflies.

INTO THE GARDEN

• You can employ some easy tricks to keep your butterflies permanently in the neighborhood. Painted Lady butterflies are known to find nectar in a wide variety of both garden and wild plants. They're not incredibly fussy about where they stop to eat. You want to keep in mind, however, that many hybrid flowers look really great but may have had any nectar-producing capabilities bred out of them. If you and the kids plan to grow a garden for your butterflies, ask the experts at your local garden center, nursery, or extension service about the "butterfly friendliness" of the seeds and plants you want to use.

If you have internet access and a favorite search engine like *google.com*, type in "malva plants" and choose from a long list of helpful sites for more information on and pictures of malva.

• Another way to almost guarantee that your butterflies stay close is to provide them with host plants for egg laying. The Painted Lady is much more particular about host plants for her eggs than nectar plants for her food. You'll have to make sure that there's plenty of hollyhock, malva (attractive broadleaf plants of the mallow family), lantana or thistle available when she goes looking for the ideal leaf on which to drop her eggs.

• Painted Lady butterflies don't migrate in the annual round trip sense of the word. However, population pressures, food supply, and even Spring weather patterns can cause them to move from place to place in huge swarms. In milder locations they can winter-over in any of the 4 stages of development since lower temperatures mean slow growth. When the weather warms and there's more sunlight, they'll take up where they left off.

• Painted Lady butterflies are found all over the world (except New Zealand, Australia and Antarctica) and have a variety of local names. Since this is true for most living things, a biologist in one part of the world has to know exactly which animal or plant his colleague in another part is describing. In 1758, a Swede named Carolus Linneaus developed a system based on the history, structures, and breeding characteristics of the plant or animal in question. He used Latin because it was universally known at the time and, more importantly, was no longer growing or evolving as a language, i.e., its rules of grammar wouldn't be changing over time. For those who are into such things, the scientific classification of a Painted Lady butterfly is:

<u>Kingdom</u>:	Animal	[you know, *animal*]
<u>Phylum</u>:	Arthropoda	[*arth-rópp-uh-dah*]
<u>Class</u>:	Insecta	[*in-séc-tah*]
<u>Order</u>:	Lepidoptera	[*lepp-ih-dóp-ter-ah*]
<u>Family</u>:	Nymphalidae	[*nim-fál-ah-dee*]
<u>Genus</u>:	Vanessa	[the girl's name!]
<u>Species</u>:	cardui	[*cárd-ewe-eye*]

• You and the kids may find these websites both useful and interesting as you work with your Painted Lady butterflies:

•Painted Lady Butterfly
mamba.bio.uci.edu/~pjbryant/biodiv/lepidopt/nymph/plady.htm

•The Red Admiral and Painted Lady Research Site
www.public.iastate.edu/~mariposa/homepage.html

•Butterflies and Their Larval Food Plants
mamba.bio.uci.edu/~pjbryant/biodiv/bflyplnt.htm

INTO THE GARDEN

• You'll want to promote the day of the release, especially with younger kids. They'll want to get everyone involved so you may even have parents in on the activity. You definitely want to encourage cameras of all kinds to record the big moment because it will be unique and memorable for everyone. Pictures of all the reactions to the butterflies are great!

• A phrase you'll hear for days and even weeks afterwards is "That's my butterfly!" Whether it's a Painted Lady or not, the younger kids will be convinced that the butterflies they raised have paid them a visit. Older kids may be more skeptical about it but may realize the fluttering visitor is perhaps the offspring of the original batch. It's a fun connection for them to make!

• The Painted Lady butterfly is found everywhere in North America. For over 30 years, releases of Painted Lady butterflies from Insect Lore have become an important part of nearly every school system in this country. They're clean, healthy and graceful, and are welcomed everywhere as pollinators and beautifiers.

• Once the butterflies have been released, cleaning the Pavilion is easy. Just rinse it by hand in warm, sudsy water then, hang it up to let it air-dry before putting it away. Then again, raising butterflies doesn't have to be just a yearly event. A new batch of caterpillars is always available year-round from Insect Lore.

WORD POWER

Here's a word (hook) you might want to have handy and use during this activity. Doing this could help keep everyone using the same hooks as the discoveries unfold.

ecosystem

WORD POWER

antenna or antennae [*an-tén-knee*]

butterfly

caterpillar

change

chrysalis [*krís-ah-liss*]

cold blooded

compare / comparison

concentration

cremaster

crochets

data

dissolve

ecosystem

emerge / emergence

entomology / entomologist

environment

frass

gravity

growing / growth

habitat / home

insect

instinct

involuntary

larva / larvae [*lár-vee*]

life / life cycle

living / non-living

meconium [*meh-kóe-knee-um*]

molt

Nature / natural

needs of living things

nutrient

observe / observations

ocelli [*oh-sél-eye*]

pheromone [*fáir-uh-moan*]

proboscis [*pro-bóss-iss*]

prolegs

pupa [*péw-pah*]

response

segments

setae [*sée-tee*]

silk

spiracles [*spéar-uh-kuls*]

solution

survival

tarsi [*tár-see*]

temperature

thermometer

tropisms [*tróe-piz-ums*]

variable

HOMES IN A CLASSROOM

GETTING STARTED

Like all living things, your caterpillar must have water, food and shelter to survive. If it lives outdoors, the habitat supplies all it needs. In a classroom, you have to supply everything. The cup isn't exactly a habitat since caterpillars aren't usually found living inside cups, but it's a safe, substitute home.

1. Preparing the 1-oz home for the caterpillar is easy. Scoop a generous half-teaspoonful of food into the cup.

2. Using the bottom of an empty 1-oz cup as a press, push the food firmly and evenly into the bottom of the cup. Try not to squish out too much water.

3. When you're finished, there should be a quarter-inch of pressed food in the cup. It's very important that the food be pushed firmly into the bottom of the cup. This protects the caterpillar in case the cup gets dropped.

4. Your teacher will probably help you by carefully placing a caterpillar inside the cup before you snap the lid on top.

5. There's plenty of air in the cup so you <u>don't</u> have to punch holes in it. Keep the caterpillar inside all the time with the lid on the cup. Warming the cup (like holding it too long, leaving it in direct sunlight, or placing it by a heat source) isn't a good idea since you don't want moisture to form on the inside walls of the cup.

6. Your teacher will have more ideas for you about how to take care of and watch your caterpillar during the next few days.

A scientist collects data by watching, measuring, comparing and writing. Start collecting data about your caterpillar on the first day you have it.

On what date did you receive your caterpillar? _____

What does your caterpillar need to stay alive? _____

_____

When do you start to see tiny threads inside the cup? Where are they?

_____

Draw what you see inside your cup when you first look at it from the side.

Use these words with this activity:

butterfly

caterpillar

change

chrysalis [krís-ah-liss]

growing / growth

habitat / home

insect

larva / larvae [lár-vee]

life / living

life cycle

living / non-living

Nature / natural

needs of living things

nutrient

observe / observations

CATERPILLAR ID

GETTING ACQUAINTED

Caterpillars grow very fast and as yours gets bigger, you'll have a better view of more and more parts on its body. You can use this activity to help you know what each part is and how the caterpillar uses it.

1. A scientist often follows the same steps each time an observation is made. For example, each time you observe your caterpillar for changes, start at its head and look at each segment in order and when you look into the cup, start at the top and work your way down. There are many things to see that may seem strange to you but are very important to the caterpillar.

2. Talk with your lab partner or teacher about what you see. Describe or draw what you're looking at as accurately as you can. Share some ideas about what it is and how the caterpillar might use it.

3. Listen carefully to the ideas your lab partner has about what something might be and where it was seen on the caterpillar. See if the two of you can find the same part on both caterpillars and then talk about how the caterpillar might need or use it.

These illustrations show caterpillars that are about 10 days old. Some of the protective bristles have been removed so you can identify the parts more easily. Some of the small parts might be hard to see but keep trying. It's really exciting to see the jaws move or to find all of the shiny, black simple eyes. Use the words below to label the pictures. Your teacher may help you fill in some of them so observe and listen carefully.

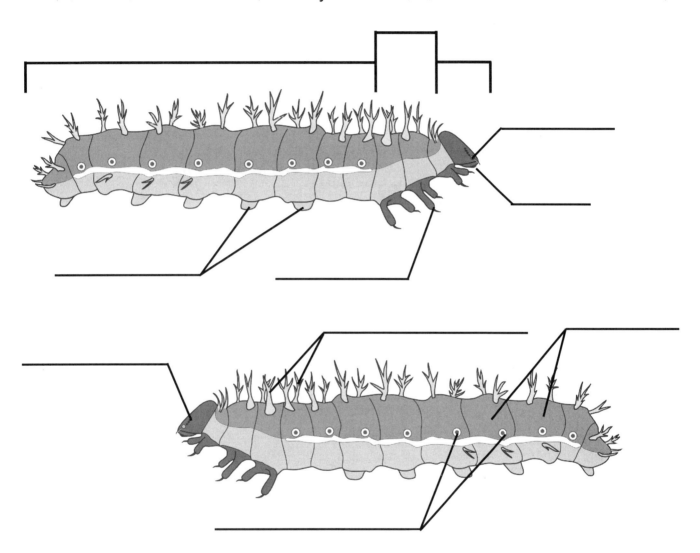

Use these words with this activity:

abdomen

antennae

breathing holes

false legs

head

jaws

simple eyes

protective bristles

segments

true legs

thorax

CATERPILLAR ID

NAME _____   DATE _____

EATING MACHINES

A SEE-FOOD DIET

Caterpillars are almost always eating and growing! Use the illustrations below to draw pictures of the changes you see in your caterpillar. To help you see it better, your teacher may show you the inside of one of the extra caterpillar cups. It's best to keep the lid closed on the cup where your caterpillar lives.

1. Pretend you've taken the lid off of your cup and you're looking into it from right above it. The smaller circle on these pictures is the food that's on the bottom of your cup. The larger circle is the cup itself.

2. Observe your caterpillar on the first day you receive it and write the date on the line below the first picture. Draw a wiggly line on the food circle that shows the length and size of your caterpillar.

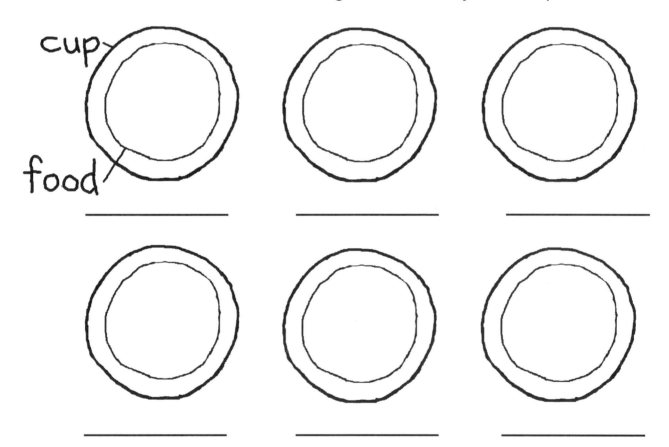

3. Make more observations of your caterpillar during the next few days. Be sure to write the date of your observation on the line under the picture. You'll see your caterpillar getting longer and bigger!

Use these pictures to show changes that you see happening in the cup. As your caterpillar grows, there will be things that are new and different. Your teacher may help you find them at first but as you observe the cup each day, you'll see more and more of them on your own. Be sure to write the date below each picture when you make your observation.

Use these words with this activity:

compare / comparison   molt
crochets   silk
data   spinneret
frass   tarsi [tár-sy]
instar

THE BUTTERFLY'S TURN

FINALLY!

This is the big moment! You waited while the caterpillar grew, made a mess in the cup, transformed into a chrysalis, and finally emerged as a butterfly. It's easy to see some amazing changes. This page will help you find them.

1. Your teacher will probably help you label the pictures above. Talk with your lab partner about the parts you see on the butterflies. Also, look closely at the colors and patterns you see from both above and below the wings. What designs and colors are the same?

2. The butterflies shown here are a little larger than real Painted Lady butterflies. The usual measurement from one wing tip across to the other wing tip is about 2 inches. What's the "wing span" for the butterflies above?

You've probably been watching your butterfly long enough to draw a pretty good picture of it. Here are 3 steps you can use to make it easy. The one on the left is the view from above and the one on the right is from below. Draw the shape of the wings carefully since this shape can often tell you what kind of butterfly it is. You can add veins to the wings to make them more real looking, too. Draw your butterfly with the 3 body parts connected.

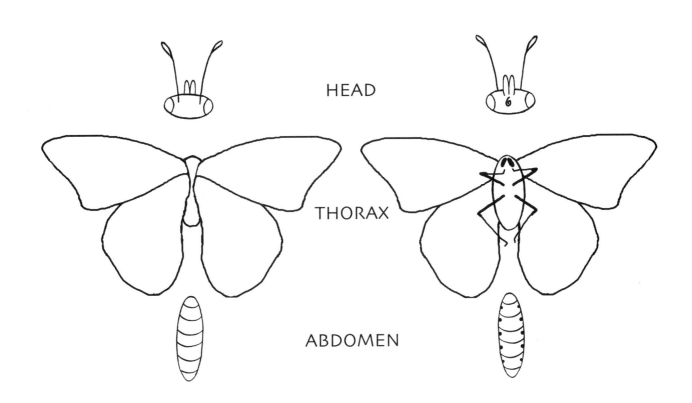

HEAD

THORAX

ABDOMEN

<u>Use these words with this activity:</u>

abdomen

antennae

breathing holes

compound eyes

fore wings

head

hind wings

meconium

pro-legs

proboscis [pro-bóss-iss]

segments

thorax

true legs

wing veins

THE BUTTERFLY'S TURN

INTO THE GARDEN

THE BIG DAY

You've had a chance to see how a caterpillar grows and becomes a butterfly and maybe you've even held a living butterfly. Painted Lady butterflies live only 2 to 4 weeks so now it's time to add them to your neighborhood and let others enjoy them, too.

1. It's best to release your butterflies on a sunny day that's about 75°F and not too windy. Your teacher will choose a spot that's probably in a garden or near some trees and bushes.

2. You may be asked to just watch or to pick up and release a butterfly. Which ever it is, you'll be part of a wonderful experience. Some of the butterflies may not fly away immediately and may land on you or near you. That's especially true if you're wearing darker, subdued colors like blue or green. However, black is a color to avoid if you want butterflies to land on you.

These bigger-than-normal outlines of a Painted Lady butterfly give you a chance to add colors to the wings and body. You may want to color them realistically so you have a reminder of your experience with live butterflies.

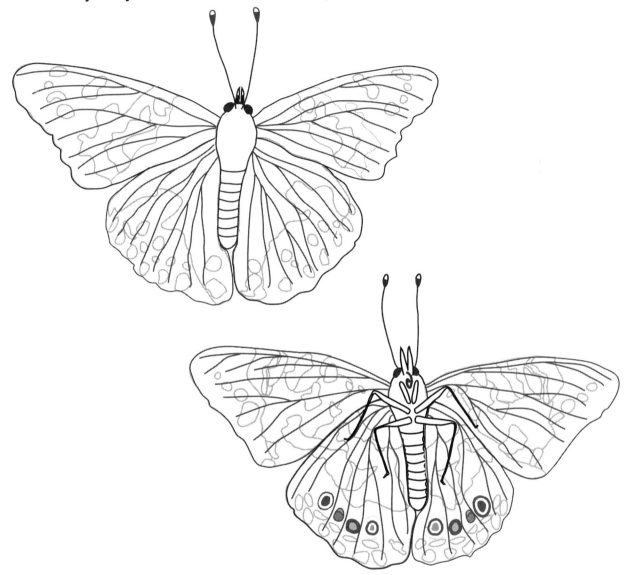

All living things make changes to their environment and influence their habitat. Share some ideas about a few good and a few not so good changes that humans have made to their habitats and to the Earth. Then, talk about some changes that have occurred on Earth that have <u>not</u> been caused by humans.

Watching a caterpillar grow and become a butterfly is a tiny change that almost always happens out-of-sight in Nature. You saw it happen right before your eyes and now it might be something you'll want to experience again and again.

Notes

Notes

Notes

Notes

Notes

Notes

Notes